CYRANO DE BERGERAC

CYRANO
DE BERGERAC

BY

EDMOND ROSTAND

TRANSLATED BY
BRIAN HOOKER

INTRODUCTION BY
CLAYTON HAMILTON

THE MODERN LIBRARY · NEW YORK

Random House IS THE PUBLISHER OF

THE MODERN LIBRARY

BENNETT A. CERF · DONALD S. KLOPFER · ROBERT K. HAAS

Manufactured in the United States of America

Printed by Parkway Printing Company   Bound by H. Wolff

*It was to the soul of CYRANO that
I intended to dedicate this poem.*

*But since that soul has been reborn
in you, COQUELIN, it is to you that I
dedicate it.*

E. R.

(The first four Acts in 1640; the fifth in 1655.)

FIRST ACT: A Performance at the Hôtel de Bourgogne.

SECOND ACT: The Bakery of the Poets.

THIRD ACT: Roxane's Kiss.

FOURTH ACT: The Cadets of Gascoyne.

FIFTH ACT: Cyrano's Gazette.

THE PERSONS

Cyrano de Bergerac
Christian de Neuvillette
Comte de Guiche
Ragueneau
Le Bret
Carbon de Castel-Jaloux
The Cadets
Lignière
Vicomte de Valvert
A Marquis
Second Marquis
Third Marquis
Montfleury
Bellerose
Jodelet
Cuigy
Brissaille
A Meddler
A Musketeer
Another Musketeer
A Spanish Officer
A Cavalier

The Porter
A Citizen
His Son
A Cut-Purse
A Spectator
A Sentry
Bertrandou the Fifer
A Capuchin
Two Musicians
The Poets
The Pastrycooks
The Pages
Roxane
Her Duenna
Lise
The Orange-Girl
Mother Marguérite de Jésus
Sister Marthe
Sister Claire
An Actress
A Soubrette
The Flower-Girl

The Crowd, Citizens, Marquis, Musketeers, Thieves, Pastrycooks, Poets, Cadets of Gascoyne, Actors, Violins, Pages, Children, Spanish Soldiers, Spectators, Intellectuals, Academicians, Nuns, etc.

PREFACE

"VOICI LES CADETS DE GASCOGNE!" . . .

(A Prefatory Gesture)

Many years ago the late Augustin Daly made a brief revival in New York of *Love's Labor's Lost,* the earliest and in most respects the poorest of the plays of Shakespeare. There had been no public demand for the piece; there was no popular approval of the presentation: but, when a friend asked Mr. Daly why he had spent his money in such an undertaking, the manager replied, "My brother, the Judge, had never seen the play and asked me for an opportunity to have a look at it."

I had this anecdote in mind when, after enduring two decades of unremitted theatre-going made dreary by the absence from our stage of the most intoxicating play of modern times, I asked Walter Hampden to let me have another look at *Cyrano de Bergerac.* This request called for the raising of many thousands of dollars, the renting of a theatre in New York, the selection and long training of a company educated to speak verse and skilled in the rendition of romantic drama, the preparation of an elaborate production, and the study and composition of one of the most exacting parts in the entire history of the stage; but I had an altruistic argument to support an appeal that had been, in the first place, merely personal. *"Cyrano,"* I said, "has not been shown in New York for nearly a quarter of a century, except at one or two negligible matinées. This means, though it is hard for us to realize the fact, that all our theatre-goers under thirty years of age have been robbed of an experience that we ourselves remember as one of the most tingling of our 'teens. I want to see *Cyrano* again; but I am thinking also of the thousands of younger people who have never seen it at all. Won't you give them a chance?"

Not wishing me to carry my grey hairs in sorrow to an early grave, Mr. Hampden generously said, "I'll do the play for you if you will find me a translation. I have never read one." "Neither have I," I answered; for both of us had been bilingual since boyhood and our enthusiasm for Rostand had been derived entirely from our early habit of chanting his bravura passages in the French original. But if Mr. Hampden was not to be daunted by the difficulties of production, I was not to be put off by the problem of an English text. "Study the part in French," I said, "and ask Claude Bragdon to design the scenery. Meanwhile, I'll get you a translation."

After a visit to a bookstore, I read, for the first time in my life, half a dozen translations into English of *Cyrano de Bergerac;* and I hope that I shall never again experience so miserable a sense of disillusionment. One or two of them were so bad that they were not worth the paper they had been printed on. Two were more than tolerable; but, though fairly faithful to the letter of the French original, they seemed to me to miss entirely its spirit. The zest, the fire, the spontaneity, the brilliancy, the lyric rapture of Rostand were lacking. I felt as annoyed as a musician condemned to listen to the murder of a composition of Mozart's by a child at the piano, continually striking sharp or flat; and, by no effort of my inward ear, could I imagine Mr. Hampden, accustomed as he was to the lines of *Hamlet* and *Othello,* speaking such pedestrian and uninspired English in a poetic part that had been written by Rostand for the incomparable voice of Coquelin.

But if Walter Hampden was willing to let me have a look at the play, it seemed only fair for me to ask another of my friends to make a translation which Mr. Hampden should be able to speak and I should be able to read. I went to Brian Hooker. I asked him abruptly if he had ever read a translation of *Cyrano de Bergerac;* and, on receiving the expected negative response, I assured him that his estate was the more gracious. I then informed him that it was his duty to drop whatever he was doing, retire to the country for a couple of months, and translate *Cyrano* for Walter Hampden. Thus, in this practical age, are poets pestered by their friends.

Since that is the way in which this new version of *Cyrano de Bergerac* happened to be undertaken, the translator and the actor-manager have asked me to introduce the text to the reading public with a prefatory gesture. I am happy, indeed, to do so; for whatever may be the fate of the revival with the theatre-going public [this preface being written necessarily in advance of the event] I know already that Brian Hooker has succeeded in a literary task of extraordinary difficulty, that he has written a text which is both speakable and readable, and that he has made the vivid spirit of Edmond Rostand accessible, for the first time in a quarter of a century, to English-reading lovers of *belles-lettres* who are not able to read French.

Mr. Hooker has asked me to explain the principles he had in mind in undertaking this new version. In the first place, since he was making it directly for production on the stage and only incidentally for publication, he wrote it by the ear and for the ear. While preserving the metres and the rhyme-schemes of the incidental lyrics, he chose blank verse as the medium for the dialogue, because, of course, the Alexandrine couplet would have sounded too outlandish to our theatre-going public. His verse is brisk, succinct, and crystal clear: it is easy for the actors to speak, and it is easy for the audience to understand without a moment's hesitance. It was far from Mr. Hooker's purpose to write a literal translation,—the sort of rendering which, plodding faithfully from word to word, might be used as a "trot" by high-school students cramming for an examination in the French original. Not a line has been omitted from Rostand's text, and not a line has been added to it. It is not to be thought for a moment that either Mr. Hooker or Mr. Hampden would have presumed to alter the play in any detail, even though such sacrilege has often been committed under the *camouflage* of "adaptation"; but, in rendering many lines and speeches, the American poet has paraphrased the French original, instead of translating it *verbatim*. He has allowed himself this liberty in order to convey more clearly to Mr. Hampden's audience the theatrical thrust or the poetical point intended by

Rostand. For instance, in the Ballade of the Duel, there is a line which reads, in the original, *"Elégant comme Céladon"*; but, knowing that nobody in an American audience could be expected to have heard of Céladon, Mr. Hooker has substituted an allusion to Sir Launcelot, a hero whom Cyrano himself might have mentioned just as naturally as a symbol of the chivalrous and courtly. Only to pedants who know nothing of the necessities of the theatre will such a process seem unscholarly; but there may be, in our universities, a few undramatic critics for whom it will be necessary to explain that Mr. Hampden, while fighting a duel and improvising a ballade, cannot pause to step down to the footlights and issue a literary footnote to the audience. And those members of the American audience who are scholarly enough to recognize, in Cyrano's bravura speech about his nose, a delightful phrase from Marlowe's *Dr. Faustus,* will know that this has been substituted for a French quotation which was equally familiar to the Parisian audience. On the one hand, it is not unlikely that the actual Cyrano, who was both a playwright and a scholar, was familiar with Marlowe's address to Helen; and, on the other hand, the American auditor would have received no kick from a literal translation of the French quotation used in the original.

To sum the matter up, Mr. Hooker was commissioned, not to write a text-book or a "trot," but to write a play and a poem. His thought, like that of Rostand before him, was always of the theatre, always of the actor, always of the audience; and that, I believe, is the reason why the

English text has turned alive under his hands and kindled itself into a veritable poem. It conveys from one language to another the briskness, the brilliance, the eloquence, the spontaneity, the rapture of the original. To me it affords a pleasure that, until this year, I had never hoped to experience,—the pleasure of reading an English version of *Cyrano de Bergerac* which could really remind me of the keen delight with which I first read the French original a quarter of a century ago.

Since I have had no part in this undertaking, except to persuade one of my friends to revive the play and another of my friends to translate the text, I might—were I so minded—say, with Cyrano,—

> *"Pendant que je restais en bas, dans l'ombre noire,*
> *D'autres montaient cueillir le baiser de la gloire!"*

But the only "kiss of glory" that any of the three of us desires is the hope of suggesting to a new generation of American play-goers and American readers a little of that rapture which we ourselves, now men of forty, derived from seeing and from reading *Cyrano de Bergerac* in the brave days of Richard Mansfield and Constant Coquelin, when we were in our 'teens.

Lucky were the lads who were growing up to manhood when *Cyrano* was written; for those were brave days indeed and the world was not yet out of joint. It was the time of the Spanish-American War, a knightly contest for a noble cause, in which we were fighting against gentlemen, not Germans; and the customs of mankind had not become so sullied as to make a chivalrous gesture seem, in that quaint phrase of Sir Thomas Browne's, "a vanity out of date and superannuated piece of folly." The year was all a-kindle with great gestures. An American officer, self-reliant and alone, attained immortal anonymity by carrying his message to Garcia. Dewey, in the early morning, steamed past anchored mines into the harbor of Manila, curved away from the Spanish fleet in order to give his seamen time for breakfast, circled back again, and with the quiet phrase, "You may fire when you are ready, Gridley," raised the United States from a provincial nation to one of the great powers of the world. Hobson made his gallant attempt to bottle up the hostile fleet at Santiago; and when, subsequently, the Spanish ships escaped and were beached and shattered in a running fight, our seamen cried, "Don't cheer, boys; the poor fellows are dying," and rushed to the rescue of the enemies they had disarmed. There is only one word for occurrences like that. It is the word of Cyrano,—"*Quel geste!*"

It was in those stirring days that *Cyrano de Bergerac* was first produced in Paris, at the *Théâtre de la Porte Saint-Martin,* on the night of December 28, 1897, and swiftly took the theatre of the world by storm. No other play in history, before or since, has ever attained a popular success so instantaneous and so enormous. Though I was only sixteen years old at the time, I can still remember clearly the noise of that first news—heard all around the rolling globe—that a young Frenchman, only twenty-nine years of age, whose name, outside of Paris, nobody had ever heard before, had written the most entrancing

and contagious play that had ever yet been shown at any
time on any stage.

In one of my books I have mentioned what this meant
to me; and, since my own experience must tally with that
of many other people who are not too young to remember
nor so old as to forget, it may not be inappropriate to
repeat it in this place. While travelers returning overseas
whetted our appetite with ecstatic accounts of *Cyrano*, we
who waited in America were stimulated to a feverish ex-
citement. I put in an order at Brentano's for the text and
bothered the bookstore for days and days and weeks and
weeks until the first copies came to us across the ocean. I
remember vaguely that there was a rather long delay, due
doubtless to some accident of printing; and I can recollect
my consequent delight at securing one of the first copies
that were delivered in this country.

In those days there was a shabby little nook in Sixth
Avenue—on the east side, just south of Twenty-Eighth
Street—that was known as the Café de Bordeaux. It was a
dingy place, frequented by impoverished Frenchmen who
played backgammon on decaying boards or ancient gam-
bling games with dirty decks of cards. Thither—at that
moment, a quarter of a century ago—I made my way,
with my virgin copy of *Cyrano de Bergerac* protruding
from my pocket. I was set upon at once, and made to open
up the book, and forced to read aloud what **every one**
was waiting for:——

> *Je jette avec grâce mon feutre,*
> *Je fais lentement l'abandon*

Du grand manteau qui me calfeutre,
Et je tire mon espadon . . .

In a moment or two the games of backgammon ceased and the whispering of falling cards was quenched in silence. I was soon enthroned upon a table and reading—in my rhetorical schoolboyish manner—the sonorous series of triolets beginning:——

Ce sont les cadets de Gascogne,
De Carbon de Castel-Jaloux! . . .

At the end of the first stanza that helter-skelter company of Frenchmen far from home broke spontaneously into cheers. I enjoyed my first and only triumph as an actor. That day within that place men played no more. . . .

Thereafter, evening after evening, Walter Hampden and I used to squander the after-midnight gas, reading and rereading the magic text of this entrancing play; and it is pleasant now to think that innumerable other boys whom we have never met were rendered sleepless at the same time by the same romantic stimulus. We were not critical in those days. We did not bother to compare Rostand with Shakespeare or Euripides or Molière. We knew only that his heroic comedy was thrillingly theatrical and that his verse was dazzling and exquisitely lyrical. That was enough for us; and that, I believe, will be enough for the younger people of the present generation when they are brought face to face with *Cyrano.*

When the news of the incomparable success of the new

piece at the *Porte Saint-Martin* had been authenticated, Richard Mansfield, the foremost American actor of the time, closed his season, slipped quietly across the ocean, and sat night after night watching from the front the performance of Constant Coquelin. Mansfield was the first actor that I saw in the part. I attended his opening at the Garden Theatre in New York, on October 3, 1898, and saw him subsequently several times during the course of that season and the next. Coquelin I did not see until the autumn of 1900, when he appeared in New York, at the same Garden Theatre, with Sarah Bernhardt as Roxane; but I made up for my delay by attending every performance in the first week of the engagement.

I am able to testify that Mansfield's *Cyrano* was not, by any means, an imitation of Coquelin's. It was, indeed, deliberately different; and, in many technical respects, it was more obviously meritorious. Mansfield's performance was more clever, more ingenious, more astonishing. But despite the cleverness of Mansfield, I preferred the performance of Coquelin. I am sure, now, that Coquelin was greater, for the simple reason that I find it more difficult, after more than twenty years, to remember what Coquelin did at any questionable moment than to remember what Mansfield did. Mansfield *acted* the part admirably; but Coquelin walked on, and *was* Cyrano, and that was the only fact to be regarded.

We cannot call back Coquelin and Mansfield and Rostand from their graves; but this gallant play is still as thrillingly alive as it was in 1898. Rostand was like Shakespeare in one respect at least; for he wrote "not of an age but for all time." It is only the realists, who write about contemporary manners and contemporary morals, who grow speedily old-fashioned: the romantics, who escape from their own period, remain forever young and ever new. And it does seem to be a great pity that, because of the faulty organization of our theatre, such a play as *Cyrano de Bergerac* should be banished from our stage for decades at a time. It is to be hoped that Mr. Hampden will keep this piece in his repertory for many years to come. Meanwhile, his revival of *Cyrano* has at least inspired Mr. Hooker to write an English version which all lovers of *belles-lettres* will accept with gratitude.

CLAYTON HAMILTON

NEW YORK CITY: OCTOBER, 1923.

THE FIRST ACT

A PERFORMANCE AT THE HÔTEL DE BOURGOGNE

CYRANO DE BERGERAC

THE HALL OF THE HÔTEL DE BOURGOGNE in 1640. *A sort of Tennis Court, arranged and decorated for Theatrical productions.*

The Hall is a long rectangle; we see it diagonally, in such a way that one side of it forms the back scene, which begins at the First Entrance on the Right and runs up to the Last Entrance on the Left, where it makes a right angle with the Stage which is seen obliquely.

This Stage is provided on either hand with benches placed along the wings. The curtain is formed by two lengths of Tapestry which can be drawn apart. Above a Harlequin cloak, the Royal Arms. Broad steps lead from the Stage down to the floor of the Hall. On either side of these steps, a place for the Musicians. A row of candles serves as footlights. Two tiers of Galleries along the side of the Hall; the upper one divided into boxes.

There are no seats upon the Floor, which is the actual stage of our theatre; but toward the back of the Hall, on the right, a few benches are arranged; and underneath a stairway on the extreme right, which leads up to the galleries, and of which only the lower portion is visible, there is a sort of Sideboard, decorated with little tapers, vases of flowers, bottles and glasses, plates of cake, et cetera.

Farther along, toward the centre of our stage, is the

3

Entrance to the Hall: a great double door which opens only slightly to admit the Audience. On one of the panels of this door, as also in other places about the Hall, and in particular just over the Sideboard, are Playbills in red, upon which we may read the title LA CLORISE.

As the CURTAIN RISES, *the Hall is dimly lighted and still empty. The Chandeliers are lowered to the floor, in the middle of the Hall, ready for lighting.*

> *(Sounds of voices outside the door. Then a Cavalier enters abruptly.)*

THE PORTER

(Follows him)

Hallo there!—Fifteen sols!

THE CAVALIER

       I enter free.

THE PORTER

Why?

THE CAVALIER

Soldier of the Household of the King!

THE PORTER

(Turns to another Cavalier who has just entered.)

You?

SECOND CAVALIER

I pay nothing.

THE PORTER

      Why not?

SECOND CAVALIER

            Musketeer!

FIRST CAVALIER

(*To the Second*)

The play begins at two. Plenty of time—
And here's the whole floor empty. Shall we try
Our exercise?

(*They fence with the foils which they have brought.*)

A LACKEY

(*Enters*)

—Pst! . . . Flanquin! . . .

ANOTHER

(*Already on stage*)

What, Champagne?

FIRST LACKEY

(*Showing games which he takes out of his doublet*)

Cards. Dice. Come on.

(*Sits on the floor*)

SECOND LACKEY

(*Same action*)

Come on, old cock!

FIRST LACKEY

(*Takes from his pocket a bit of candle, lights it, sets it on the floor.*)

I have stolen
A little of my master's fire.

A GUARDSMAN

(*To a flower girl who comes forward*)

How sweet

Of you, to come before they light the hall!
(*Puts his arm around her.*)

FIRST CAVALIER
(*Receives a thrust of the foil*)
A hit!

SECOND LACKEY
A club!

THE GUARDSMAN
(*Pursuing the girl*)
A kiss!

THE FLOWER GIRL
(*Pushing away from him*)
They'll see us!—

THE GUARDSMAN
(*Draws her into a dark corner*)
No danger!

A MAN
(*Sits on the floor, together with several others who
have brought packages of food*)
When we come early, we have time to eat.

A CITIZEN
(*Escorting his son, a boy of sixteen*)
Sit here, my son.

FIRST LACKEY
Mark the Ace!

ANOTHER MAN
(*Draws a bottle from under his cloak and sits down
with the others*)

                              Here's the spot
For a jolly old sot to suck his Burgundy—
      (*Drinks*)
Here—in the house of the Burgundians!

THE CITIZEN

      (*To his son*)
Would you not think you were in some den of vice?
      (*Points with his cane at the drunkard*)
Drunkards—
      (*In stepping back, one of the cavaliers trips him up*)
                  Bullies!—
      (*He falls between the lackeys*)
                        Gamblers!—

THE GUARDSMAN

      (*Behind him as he rises, still struggling with the
      Flower Girl*)
                              One kiss—

THE CITIZEN

                        Good God!—

      (*Draws his son quickly away*)
Here!—And to think, my son, that in this hall
They play Rotrou!

THE BOY

                  Yes, father—and Corneille!

THE PAGES

      (*Dance in, holding hands and singing:*)
Tra-la-la-la-la-la-la-la-la-lère . . .

THE PORTER

You pages there—no nonsense!

FIRST PAGE

(*With wounded dignity*)

                   Oh, Monsieur!

Really! How could you?

(*To the Second, the moment the Porter turns
his back*)

                   Pst!—a bit of string?

SECOND PAGE

(*Shows fishline with hook*)

Yes—and a hook.

FIRST PAGE

               Up in the gallery,

And fish for wigs!

A CUT-PURSE

(*Gathers around him several evil-looking young
fellows*)

                Now then, you picaroons,

Perk up, and hear me mutter. Here's your bout—
Bustle around some cull, and bite his bung . . .

SECOND PAGE

(*Calls to other pages already in the gallery*)

Hey! Brought your pea-shooters?

THIRD PAGE

(*From above*)

                   And our peas, too!

(*Blows, and showers them with peas*)

THE BOY

What is the play this afternoon?

THE CITIZEN

Clorise.

THE BOY

Who wrote that?

THE CITIZEN

Balthasar Baro. What a play! . . .

(He takes The Boy's arm and leads him up-stage)

THE CUT-PURSE

(To his pupils)

Lace now, on those long sleeves, you cut it off—

(Gesture with thumb and finger, as if using scissors)

A SPECTATOR

(To another, pointing upward toward the gallery)

Ah, *Le Cid!*—Yes, the first night, I sat there—

THE CUT-PURSE

Watches—

(Gesture as of picking a pocket)

THE CITIZEN

(Coming down with his son)

Great actors we shall see to-day—

THE CUT-PURSE

Handkerchiefs—

(Gesture of holding the pocket with left hand, and drawing out handkerchief with right)

THE CITIZEN

Montfleury—

A VOICE

(*In the gallery*)

Lights! Light the lights!

THE CITIZEN

Bellerose, l'Épy, Beaupré, Jodelet—

A PAGE

(*On the floor*)

Here comes the orange-girl.

THE ORANGE-GIRL

Oranges, milk,

Raspberry syrup, lemonade—
(*Noise at the door*)

A FALSETTO VOICE

(*Outside*)

Make way,

Brutes!

FIRST LACKEY

What, the Marquis—on the floor?
(*The Marquis enters in a little group.*)

SECOND LACKEY

Not long—

Only a few moments; they'll go and sit
On the stage presently.

FIRST MARQUIS

(*Seeing the hall half empty*)

How now! We enter

Like tradespeople—no crowding, no disturbance!—
No treading on the toes of citizens?

Oh fie! Oh fie!

> (*He encounters two gentlemen who have already arrived*)
>
> Cuigy! Brissaille!
>
> (*Great embracings*)

CUIGY

The faithful!

> (*Looks around him*)

We are here before the candles.

FIRST MARQUIS

Ah, be still!

You put me in a temper.

SECOND MARQUIS

Console yourself,

Marquis—The lamplighter!

THE CROWD

> (*Applauding the appearance of the lamplighter*)
> Ah! . . .
>
> (*A group gathers around the chandelier while he lights it. A few people have already taken their place in the gallery.* Lignière *enters the hall, arm in arm with* Christian de Neuvillette. Lignière *is a slightly disheveled figure, dissipated and yet distinguished looking.* Christian, *elegantly but rather unfashionably dressed, appears pre-occupied and keeps looking up at the boxes.*)

CUIGY

Lignière!—

BRISSAILLE

(Laughing)

Still sober—at this hour?

LIGNIÈRE

(To CHRISTIAN*)*

May I present you?

*(*CHRISTIAN *assents.)*

Baron Christian de Neuvillette.

(They salute.)

THE CROWD

(Applauding as the lighted chandelier is hoisted into place)

Ah!—

CUIGY

(Aside to BRISSAILLE, *looking at* CHRISTIAN*)*

Rather

A fine head, is it not? The profile . . .

FIRST MARQUIS

(Who has overheard)

Peuh!

LIGNIÈRE

(Presenting them to CHRISTIAN*)*

Messieurs de Cuigy . . . de Brissaille . . .

CHRISTIAN

(Bows)   Enchanted!

FIRST MARQUIS

(To the second)

He is not ill-looking; possibly a shade
Behind the fashion.

LIGNIÈRE

(*To* CUIGY)

          Monsieur is recently

From the Touraine.

CHRISTIAN

        . . .. Yes, I have been in Paris

Two or three weeks only. I join the Guards

To-morrow.

FIRST MARQUIS

(*Watching the people who come into the boxes*)
    Look—Madame la Présidente

Aubry!

THE ORANGE-GIRL

    Oranges, milk—

THE VIOLINS

(*Tuning up*)
      La . . . la . . .

CUIGY

(*To* CHRISTIAN, *calling his attention to the increasing crowd*)

                We have

An audience to-day!

CHRISTIAN

    A brilliant one.

FIRST MARQUIS

Oh, yes, all our own people—the gay world!

(*They name the ladies who enter the boxes elaborately dressed. Bows and smiles are exchanged.*)

SECOND MARQUIS

Madame de Guéméné . . .

CUIGY

De Bois-Dauphin . . .

FIRST MARQUIS

Whom we adore—

BRISSAILLE

Madame de Chavigny . . .

SECOND MARQUIS

Who plays with all our hearts—

LIGNIÈRE

Why, there's Corneille

Returned from Rouen!

THE BOY

(*To his father*)

Are the Academy

All here?

THE CITIZEN

I see some of them . . . there's Boudu—
Boissat—Cureau—Porchères—Colomby—
Bourzeys—Bourdon—Arbaut—

Ah, those great names,

Never to be forgotten!

FIRST MARQUIS

Look—at last!

Our Intellectuals! Barthénoide,
Urimédonte, Félixérie . . .

SECOND MARQUIS

(Languishing)

Sweet heaven!
How exquisite their surnames are! Marquis,
You know them all?

FIRST MARQUIS

I know them all, Marquis!

LIGNIÈRE

(Draws CHRISTIAN *aside)*
My dear boy, I came here to serve you— Well,
But where's the lady? I'll be going.

CHRISTIAN

Not yet—

A little longer! She is always here.
Please! I must find some way of meeting her.
I am dying of love! And you—you know
Everyone, the whole court and the whole town,
And put them all into your songs—at least
You can tell me her name!

THE FIRST VIOLIN

(Raps on his desk with his bow)

Pst— Gentlemen!

(Raises his bow)

THE ORANGE-GIRL

Macaroons, lemonade—

CHRISTIAN

Then she may be
One of those æsthetes . . . Intellectuals,

You call them— How can I talk to a woman
In that style? I have no wit. This fine manner
Of speaking and of writing nowadays—
Not for me! I am a soldier—and afraid.
That's her box, on the right—the empty one.

LIGNIÈRE

(*Starts for the door*)
I am going.

CHRISTIAN

(*Restrains him*)
        No—wait!

LIGNIÈRE

                    Not I. There's a tavern
Not far away—and I am dying of thirst.

THE ORANGE-GIRL

(*Passes with her tray*)
Orange juice?

LIGNIÈRE

        No!

THE ORANGE-GIRL
        Milk?

LIGNIÈRE

            Pouah!

THE ORANGE-GIRL

                    Muscatel?

LIGNIÈRE

Here! Stop!

(*To* CHRISTIAN)

I'll stay a little.

(*To the Girl*)

Let me see

Your Muscatel.

    (*He sits down by the sideboard. The Girl pours out
    wine for him.*)

VOICES

(*In the crowd about the door, upon the entrance
of a spruce little man, rather fat, with a beaming
smile*)

Ragueneau!

LIGNIÈRE

(*To* CHRISTIAN)

Ragueneau,

Poet and pastrycook—a character!

RAGUENEAU

(*Dressed like a confectioner in his Sunday clothes,
advances quickly to* LIGNIÈRE)

Sir, have you seen Monsieur de Cyrano?

LIGNIÈRE

(*Presents him to* CHRISTIAN)

Permit me . . . Ragueneau, confectioner,
The chief support of modern poetry.

RAGUENEAU

(*Bridling*)

Oh—too much honor!

LIGNIÈRE

Patron of the Arts—

Mæcenas! Yes, you are—

RAGUENEAU

Undoubtedly,

The poets gather round my hearth.

LIGNIÈRE

On credit—

Himself a poet—

RAGUENEAU

So they say—

LIGNIÈRE

Maintains

The Muses.

RAGUENEAU

It is true that for an ode—

LIGNIÈRE

You give a tart—

RAGUENEAU

A tartlet—

LIGNIÈRE

Modesty!

And for a triolet you give—

RAGUENEAU

Plain bread!

LIGNIÈRE

(*Severely*)

Bread and milk! And you love the theatre?

RAGUENEAU

I adore it!

LIGNIÈRE

Well, pastry pays for all.
Your place to-day now—Come, between ourselves,
What did it cost you?

RAGUENEAU

Four pies; fourteen cakes.

(*Looking about*)
But— Cyrano not here? Astonishing!

LIGNIÈRE

Why so?

RAGUENEAU

Why— Montfleury plays!

LIGNIÈRE

Yes, I hear

That hippopotamus assumes the rôle
Of Phédon. What is that to Cyrano?

RAGUENEAU

Have you not heard? Monsieur de Bergerac
So hates Montfleury, he has forbidden him
For three weeks to appear upon the stage.

LIGNIÈRE

(*Who is, by this time, at his fourth glass*)
Well?

RAGUENEAU

Montfleury plays!—

CUIGY

(*Strolls over to them*)

Yes—what then?

RAGUENEAU

Ah! That
Is what I came to see.

FIRST MARQUIS

This Cyrano—
Who is he?

CUIGY

Oh, he is the lad with the long sword.

SECOND MARQUIS

Noble?

CUIGY

Sufficiently; he is in the Guards.
(*Points to a gentleman who comes and goes about
the hall as though seeking for someone*)
His friend Le Bret can tell you more.
(*Calls to him*)

Le Bret!
(LE BRET *comes down to them*)
Looking for Bergerac?

LE BRET

Yes. And for trouble.

CUIGY

It he not an extraordinary man?

LE BRET

The best friend and the bravest soul alive!

RAGUENEAU

Poet—

CUIGY

Swordsman—

LE BRET

Musician—

BRISSAILLE

Philosopher—

LIGNIÈRE

Such a remarkable appearance, too!

RAGUENEAU

Truly, I should not look to find his portrait
By the grave hand of Philippe de Champagne.
He might have been a model for Callot—
One of those wild swashbucklers in a masque—
Hat with three plumes, and doublet with six points—
His cloak behind him over his long sword
Cocked, like the tail of strutting Chanticleer—
Prouder than all the swaggering Tamburlaines
Hatched out of Gascony. And to complete
This Punchinello figure—such a nose!—
My lords, there is no such nose as that nose—
You cannot look upon it without crying: "Oh, no,
Impossible! Exaggerated!" Then
You smile, and say: "Of course— I might have known;
Presently he will take it off." But that
Monsieur de Bergerac will never do.

LIGNIÈRE

(*Grimly*)

He keeps it—and God help the man who smiles!

RAGUENEAU

His sword is one half of the shears of Fate!

FIRST MARQUIS

(*Shrugs*)

He will not come.

RAGUENEAU

Will he not? Sir, I'll lay you
A pullet à la Ragueneau!

FIRST MARQUIS

(*Laughing*)

Done!

(*Murmurs of admiration;* ROXANE *has just appeared in her box. She sits at the front of the
box, and her Duenna takes a seat toward the
rear.* CHRISTIAN, *busy paying the Orange-Girl,
does not see her at first.*)

SECOND MARQUIS

(*With little excited cries*)

Ah!

Oh! Oh! Sweet sirs, look yonder! Is she not
Frightfully ravishing?

FIRST MARQUIS

Bloom of the peach—
Blush of the strawberry—

SECOND MARQUIS

So fresh—so cool,
That our hearts, grown all warm with loving her,
May catch their death of cold!

CHRISTIAN

(*Looks up, sees* ROXANE, *and seizes* LIGNIÈRE *by
the arm.*)

There! Quick—up there—
In the box! Look!—

LIGNIÈRE

(*Coolly*)

Herself?

CHRISTIAN

Quickly— Her name!

LIGNIÈRE

(*Sipping his wine, and speaking between sips*)
Madeleine Robin, called Roxane . . . refined . . .
Intellectual . . .

CHRISTIAN

Ah!—

LIGNIÈRE

Unmarried . . .

CHRISTIAN

Oh!—

LIGNIÈRE

No title . . . rich enough . . . an orphan . . . cousin
To Cyrano . . . of whom we spoke just now . . .
(*At this point, a very distinguished looking gentle-*

*man, the Cordon Bleu around his neck, enters
the box, and stands a moment talking with*
ROXANE.)

CHRISTIAN

(*Starts*)
And the man? . . .

LIGNIÈRE

(*Beginning to feel his wine a little; cocks his eye
at them.*)
Oho! That man? . . . Comte de Guiche . . .
In love with her . . . married himself, however,
To the niece of the Cardinal—Richelieu . . .
Wishes Roxane, therefore, to marry one
Monsieur de Valvert . . . Vicomte . . . friend of his . . .
A somewhat melancholy gentleman . . .
But . . . well, accommodating! . . . She says No . . .
Nevertheless, de Guiche is powerful . . .
Not above persecuting . . .
(*He rises, swaying a little, and very happy.*)
                              I have written
A little song about his little game . . .
Good little song, too . . . Here, I'll sing it for you . . .
Make de Guiche furious . . . naughty little song . . .
Not so bad, either— Listen! . . .
(*He stands with his glass held aloft, ready to sing.*)

CHRISTIAN

                                        No. Adieu.

LIGNIÈRE

Whither away?

CHRISTIAN

To Monsieur de Valvert!

LIGNIÈRE

Careful! The man's a swordsman . . .

(*Nods toward* ROXANE, *who is watching* CHRISTIAN.)

Wait! Someone

Looking at you—

CHRISTIAN

Roxane! . . .

(*He forgets everything, and stands spellbound, gazing toward* ROXANE. *The Cut-Purse and his crew, observing him transfixed, his eyes raised and his mouth half open, begin edging in his direction.*)

LIGNIÈRE

Oh! Very well,

Then I'll be leaving you . . . Good day . . . Good day! . . .

(CHRISTIAN *remains motionless.*)

Everywhere else, they like to hear me sing!—
Also, I am thirsty.

(*He goes out, navigating carefully.* LE BRET, *having made the circuit of the hall, returns to* RAGUENEAU, *somewhat reassured.*)

LE BRET

No sign anywhere

Of Cyrano!

RAGUENEAU

(*Incredulous*)
                Wait and see!

LE BRET
                        Humph! I hope
He has not seen the bill.

THE CROWD
                        The play!—The play!—

FIRST MARQUIS
(*Observing* DE GUICHE, *as he descends from* ROX-
ANE'S *box and crosses the floor, followed by a
knot of obsequious gentlemen, the* VICOMTE DE
VALVERT *among them.*)
This man de Guiche—what ostentation!

SECOND MARQUIS
                                Bah!—
Another Gascon!

FIRST MARQUIS
                Gascon, yes—but cold
And calculating—certain to succeed—
My word for it. Come, shall we make our bow?
We shall be none the worse, I promise you . . .
        (*They go toward* DE GUICHE.)

SECOND MARQUIS
Beautiful ribbons, Count! That color, now,
What is it—*Kiss-me-Dear* or *Startled-Fawn?*

DE GUICHE
I call that shade *The Dying Spaniard.*

FIRST MARQUIS

Ha!

And no false colors either—thanks to you
And your brave troops, in Flanders before long
The Spaniard will die daily.

DE GUICHE

Shall we go
And sit upon the stage? Come, Valvert.

CHRISTIAN

(Starts at the name)

Valvert!—

The Vicomte— Ah, that scoundrel! Quick—my glove—
I'll throw it in his face—

(Reaching into his pocket for his glove, he catches
the hand of the Cut-Purse)

THE CUT-PURSE

Oh!—

CHRISTIAN

(Holding fast to the man's wrist)

Who are you?

I was looking for a glove—

THE CUT-PURSE

(Cringing)

You found a hand.

(Hurriedly)
Let me go—I can tell you something—

CHRISTIAN

(Still holding him)

Well?

THE CUT-PURSE

Lignière—that friend of yours—

CHRISTIAN

(*Same business*)

Well?

THE CUT-PURSE

Good as dead—
Understand? Ambuscaded. Wrote a song
About—no matter. There's a hundred men
Waiting for him to-night—I'm one of them.

CHRISTIAN

A hundred! Who arranged this?

THE CUT-PURSE

Secret.

CHRISTIAN

Oh!

THE CUT-PURSE

(*With dignity*)
Professional secret.

CHRISTIAN

Where are they to be?

THE CUT-PURSE

Porte de Nesle. On his way home. Tell him so.
Save his life.

CHRISTIAN

(*Releases the man*)
Yes, but where am I to find him?

THE CUT-PURSE

Go round the taverns. There's the Golden Grape,
The Pineapple, The Bursting Belt, The Two
Torches, The Three Funnels—in every one
You leave a line of writing—understand?
To warn him.

CHRISTIAN

(*Starts for the door*)
                    I'll go! God, what swine—a hundred
Against one man! . . .
        (*Stops and looks longingly at* ROXANE)
                            Leave *her* here!—
        (*Savagely, turning toward* VALVERT)
                                And leave *him!*—

(*Decidedly*)
I must save Lignière!
        (*Exit*)
        (DE GUICHE, VALVERT, *and all the Marquis have
            disappeared through the curtains, to take their
            seats upon the stage. The floor is entirely filled;
            not a vacant seat remains in the gallery or in the
            boxes.*)

THE CROWD

                    The play! The play!

Begin the play!

A CITIZEN

    (*As his wig is hoisted into the air on the end of
        a fishline, in the hands of a page in the gallery*)
        My wig!!

CRIES OF JOY

He's bald! Bravo,
You pages! Ha ha ha!

THE CITIZEN

(*Furious, shakes his fist at the boy*)

Here, you young villain!

CRIES AND LAUGHTER

(*Beginning very loud, then suddenly repressed*)
HA HA! Ha Ha! ha ha. . . .
(*Complete silence*)

LE BRET

(*Surprised*)

That sudden hush! . . .
(*A Spectator whispers in his ear.*)
Yes?

THE SPECTATOR

I was told on good authority . . .

MURMURS

(*Here and there*)
What? . . . Here? . . . No . . . Yes . . . Look—in the
latticed box—
The Cardinal! . . . The Cardinal! . . .

A PAGE

The Devil!—
Now we shall all have to behave ourselves!
(*Three raps on the stage. The audience becomes
motionless. Silence*)

THE VOICE OF A MARQUIS

(*From the stage, behind the curtains*)

Snuff that candle!

ANOTHER MARQUIS

(*Puts his head out through the curtains.*)

A chair! . . .

(*A chair is passed from hand to hand over the heads
of the crowd. He takes it, and disappears behind
the curtains, not without having blown a few
kisses to the occupants of the boxes.*)

A SPECTATOR

Silence!

VOICES

Hssh! . . . Hssh! . . .

(*Again the three raps on the stage. The curtains
part.* TABLEAU. *The Marquis seated on their
chairs to right and left of the stage, insolently
posed. Back drop representing a pastoral scene,
bluish in tone. Four little crystal chandeliers light
up the stage. The violins play softly.*)

LE BRET

(*In a low tone to* RAGUENEAU)

Montfleury enters now?

RAGUENEAU

(*Nods*)

Opens the play.

LE BRET

(*Much relieved*)

Then Cyrano is not here!

RAGUENEAU

I lose . . .

LE BRET

Humph!

So much the better!

> (*The melody of a Musette is heard.* Montfleury
> *appears upon the scene, a ponderous figure in
> the costume of a rustic shepherd, a hat garlanded
> with roses tilted over one ear, playing upon a
> beribboned pastoral pipe*)

THE CROWD

(*Applauds*)

Montfleury! . . . Bravo! . . .

MONTFLEURY

> (*After bowing to the applause, begins the rôle of
> Phédon*)

"Thrice happy he who hides from pomp and power
In sylvan shade or solitary bower;
Where balmy zephyrs fan his burning cheeks—"

A VOICE

(*From the midst of the hall*)

Wretch! Have I not forbade you these three weeks?

> (*Sensation. Every one turns to look. Murmurs*)

SEVERAL VOICES

What? . . . Where? . . . Who is it? . . .

CUIGY

Cyrano!

LE BRET

(In alarm)

Himself!

THE VOICE

King of clowns! Leave the stage—*at once!*

THE CROWD

Oh!

MONTFLEURY

Now,

Now, now—

THE VOICE

You disobey me?

SEVERAL VOICES

(From the floor, from the boxes)

Hsh! Go on—

Quiet!—Go on, Montfleury!—Who's afraid?—

MONTFLEURY

(In a voice of no great assurance)
"Thrice happy he who hides from ..."

THE VOICE

(More menacingly)

Well? Well? Well? ...

Monarch of mountebanks! Must I come and plant
A forest on your shoulders?

> *(A cane at the end of a long arm shakes above the*
> *heads of the crowd.)*

MONTFLEURY

(In a voice increasingly feeble)
"Thrice hap—"
(The cane is violently agitated.)

THE VOICE

GO!!!

THE CROWD

Ah! . . .

CYRANO

(Arises in the centre of the floor, erect upon a
chair, his arms folded, his hat cocked ferociously,
his moustache bristling, his nose terrible.)
Presently I shall grow angry!
(Sensation at his appearance)

MONTFLEURY

(To the Marquis)
Messieurs,

If you protect me—

A MARQUIS

(Nonchalantly)
Well—proceed!

CYRANO

Fat swine!

If you dare breathe one balmy zephyr more,
"ll fan your cheeks for you!

THE MARQUIS

Quiet down there!

CYRANO

Unless these gentlemen retain their seats,
My cane may bite their ribbons!

ALL THE MARQUIS

(*On their feet*)

That will do!—

Montfleury—

CYRANO

Fly, goose! Shoo! Take to your wings,
Before I pluck your plumes, and draw your gorge!

A VOICE

See here!—

CYRANO

Off stage!

ANOTHER VOICE

One moment—

CYRANO

What—still there?
(*Turns back his cuffs deliberately.*)
Very good—then I enter—*Left—with knife—*
To carve this large Italian sausage.

MONTFLEURY

(*Desperately attempting dignity*)

Sir,
When you insult me, you insult the Muse!

CYRANO

(*With great politeness*)
Sir, if the Muse, who never knew your name,

Had the honor to meet you—then be sure
That after one glance at that face of yours,
That figure of a mortuary urn—
She would apply her buskin—toward the rear!

THE CROWD

Montfleury! . . . Montfleury! . . . The play! The play!

CYRANO

(To those who are shouting and crowding about
    him)

Pray you, be gentle with my scabbard here—
She'll put her tongue out at you presently!—

(The circle enlarges.)

THE CROWD

(Recoiling)

Keep back—

CYRANO

(To MONTFLEURY)
        Begone!

THE CROWD

(Pushing in closer, and growling.)
                Ahr! . . . ahr! . . .

CYRANO

(Turns upon them.)

                        Did some one speak?

(They recoil again.)

A VOICE

(In the back of the hall, sings.)
        Monsieur de Cyrano
        Must be another Cæsar—

Let Brutus lay him low,
   And play us La Clorise!

ALL THE CROWD

(*Singing*)
      La Clorise! La Clorise!

CYRANO

Let me hear one more word of that same song,
And I destroy you all!

A CITIZEN

        Who might you be?
Samson?—

CYRANO

     Precisely. Would you kindly lend me
Your jawbone?

A LADY

(*In one of the boxes*)
      What an outrage!

A NOBLE

         Scandalous!

A CITIZEN

Annoying!

A PAGE

What a game!

THE CROWD

      Kss! Montfleury!
Cyrano!

CYRANO

   Silence!

THE CROWD

(*Delirious*)

Woof! Woof! Baaa! **Cockadoo!**

CYRANO

I—

A PAGE

Meow!

CYRANO

I say be silent!—

(*His voice dominates the uproar. Momentary hush.*)

And I offer
One universal challenge to you all!
Approach, young heroes—I will take your names.
Each in his turn—no crowding! One, two, three—
Come, get your numbers—who will head the list—
You, sir? No— You? Ah, no. To the first man
Who falls I'll build a monument! . . . Not one?
Will all who wish to die, please raise their hands? . . .
I see. You are so modest, you might blush
Before a sword naked. Sweet innocence! . . .
Not one name? Not one finger? . . . Very well,
Then I go on:

(*Turning back toward the stage, where* MONT-
FLEURY *waits in despair.*)

I'd have our theatre cured
Of this carbuncle. Or if not, why then—

(*His hand on his sword hilt.*)

The lancet!

MONTFLEURY

I—

CYRANO

(*Descends from his chair, seats himself comfortably in the centre of the circle which has formed around him, and makes himself quite at home.*)
Attend to me—full moon!
I clap my hands, three times—thus. At the third
You will eclipse yourself.

THE CROWD

(*Amused*)

Ah!

CYRANO

Ready? *One.*

MONTFLEURY

I—

A VOICE

(*From the boxes*)
No!

THE CROWD

He'll go— He'll stay—

MONTFLEURY

I really think,

Gentlemen—

CYRANO

Two.

MONTFLEURY

Perhaps I had better—

CYRANO

Three!

(MONTFLEURY *disappears, as if through a trap-door.*
Tempest of laughter, hoots and hisses.)

THE CROWD

Yah!—Coward—Come back—

CYRANO

(*Beaming, drops back in his chair and crosses his*
legs)

Let him—if he dare!

A CITIZEN

The Manager! Speech! Speech!

(BELLEROSE *advances and bows.*)

THE BOXES

Ah! Bellerose!

BELLEROSE

(*With elegance*)

Most noble—most fair—

THE CROWD

No! The Comedian—

Jodelet!—

JODELET

(*Advances, and speaks through his nose.*)

Lewd fellows of the baser sort—

THE CROWD

Ha! Ha! Not bad! Bravo!

JODELET

No Bravos here!
Our heavy tragedian with the voluptuous bust
Was taken suddenly—

THE CROWD

Yah! Coward!

JODELET

I mean . .
He had to be excused—

THE CROWD

Call him back— No!—
Yes!—

THE BOY

(*To* CYRANO)

After all, Monsieur, what reason have you
To hate this Montfleury?

CYRANO

(*Graciously, still seated*)

My dear young man,
I have two reasons, either one alone
Conclusive. *Primo:* A lamentable actor,
Who mouths his verse and moans his tragedy,
And heaves up— Ugh!—like a hod-carrier, lines
That ought to soar on their own wings. *Secundo:—*
Well—that's my secret.

THE OLD CITIZEN

(*Behind him*)

But you close the play—

La Clorise—by Baro! Are we to miss
Our entertainment, merely—

CYRANO

(*Respectfully, turns his chair toward the old man*)
            My dear old boy,
The poetry of Baro being worth
Zero, or less, I feel that I have done
Poetic justice!

THE INTELLECTUALS

(*In the boxes*)
         Really!—our Baro!—
My dear!—Who ever?—Ah, dieu! The idea!—

CYRANO

(*Gallantly, turns his chair toward the boxes*)
Fair ladies—shine upon us like the sun,
Blossom like flowers around us—be our songs,
Heard in a dream— Make sweet the hour of death,
Smiling upon us as you close our eyes—
Inspired, but do not try to criticize!

BELLEROSE

Quite so!—and the mere money—possibly
You would like that returned— Yes?

CYRANO

             Bellerose,
You speak the first word of intelligence!
I will not wound the mantle of the Muse—
Here, catch!—

(*Throws him a purse*)
         And hold your tongue.

THE CROWD
(*Astonished*)

Ah! Ah!

JODELET
(*Deftly catches the purse, weighs it in his hand*)

Monsieur,

You are hereby authorized to close our play
Every night, on the same terms.

THE CROWD

Boo!

JODELET

And welcome!

Let us be booed together, you and I!

BELLEROSE

Kindly pass out quietly . . .

JODELET
(*Burlesquing* BELLEROSE)

Quietly . . .

(*They begin to go out, while* CYRANO *looks about
    him with satisfaction. But the exodus ceases
    presently during the ensuing scene. The ladies in
    the boxes who have already risen and put on
    their wraps, stop to listen, and finally sit down
    again.*)

LE BRET
(*To* CYRANO)

Idiot!

A MEDDLER

(*Hurries up to* CYRANO.)
But what a scandal! Montfluery—
The great Montfleury! Did you know the Duc
De Candale was his patron? Who is yours?

CYRANO

No one.

THE MEDDLER

No one—no patron?

CYRANO

I said no.

THE MEDDLER

What, no great lord, to cover with his name—

CYRANO

(*With visible annoyance*)
No, I have told you twice. Must I repeat?
No sir, no patron—
(*His hand on his sword*)
But a patroness!

THE MEDDLER

And when do you leave Paris?

CYRANO

That's as may be.

THE MEDDLER

The Duc de Candale has a long arm.

CYRANO

Mine

Is longer,
> (*Drawing his sword*)
>> by three feet of steel.

THE MEDDLER

Yes, yes,

But do you dream of daring—

CYRANO

I do dream

Of daring . . .

THE MEDDLER

But—

CYRANO

You may go now.

THE MEDDLER

But—

CYRANO

You may go—

Or tell me why are you staring at my nose!

THE MEDDLER

(*In confusion*)

No—I—

CYRANO

(*Stepping up to him*)
> Does it astonish you?

THE MEDDLER

(*Drawing back*)

Your grace

Misunderstands my—

CYRANO

Is it long and soft
And dangling, like a trunk?

THE MEDDLER

(*Same business*)

I never said—

CYRANO

Or crooked, like an owl's beak?

THE MEDDLER

I—

CYRANO

Perhaps
A pimple ornaments the end of it?

THE MEDDLER

No—

CYRANO

Or a fly parading up and down?
What is this portent?

THE MEDDLER

Oh!—

CYRANO

This phenomenon?

THE MEDDLER

But I have been careful not to look—

CYRANO

And why
Not, if you please?

THE MEDDLER

Why—

CYRANO

It disgusts you, then?

THE MEDDLER

My dear sir—

CYRANO

Does its color appear to you
Unwholesome?

THE MEDDLER

Oh, by no means!

CYRANO

Or its form
Obscene?

THE MEDDLER

Not in the least—

CYRANO

Then why assume
This deprecating manner? Possibly
You find it just a trifle large?

THE MEDDLER

(*Babbling*)

Oh, no!—
Small, very small, infinitesimal—

CYRANO

(*Roars*)

What!

How? You accuse me of absurdity?
Small—*my nose?* Why—

THE MEDDLER

(*Breathless*)
                    My God!—

CYRANO

                                        Magnificent,
My nose! . . . You pug, you knob, you button-head,
Know that I glory in this nose of mine,
For a great nose indicates a great man—
Genial, courteous, intellectual,
Virile, courageous—as I am—and such
As you—poor wretch—will never dare to be
Even in imagination. For that face—
That blank, inglorious concavity
Which my right hand finds—
        (*He strikes him.*)

THE MEDDLER
                    Ow!

CYRANO
                                    —on top of you,
Is as devoid of pride, of poetry,
Of soul, of picturesqueness, of contour,
Of character, of NOSE in short—as that
        (*Takes him by the shoulders and turns him around
            suiting the action to the word*)
Which at the end of that limp spine of yours
My left foot—

THE MEDDLER

(*Escaping*)
> Help! The Guard!

CYRANO

> Take notice, all
Who find this feature of my countenance
A theme for comedy! When the humorist
Is noble, then my custom is to show
Appreciation proper to his rank—
More heartfelt . . . and more pointed. . . .

DE GUICHE

(*Who has come down from the stage, surrounded
by the Marquis*)

> Presently
This fellow will grow tiresome.

VALVERT

(*Shrugs*)
> Oh, he blows
His trumpet!

DE GUICHE
> Well—will no one interfere?

VALVERT

No one?
(*Looks round*)
> Observe. I myself will proceed
To put him in his place.
(*He walks up to* CYRANO, *who has been watching
him, and stands there, looking him over with an
affected air.*)

                              Ah . . . your nose . . . hem! . . .
Your nose is . . . rather large!

CYRANO

(*Gravely*)

                              Rather.

VALVERT

(*Simpering*)

                                        Oh well—

CYRANO

(*Coolly*)
Is that all?

VALVERT

(*Turns away, with a shrug*)
        Well, of course—

CYRANO

                              Ah, no, young sir!
You are too simple. Why, you might have said—
Oh, a great many things! Mon dieu, why waste
Your opportunity? For example, thus:—
AGGRESSIVE: I, sir, if that nose were mine,
I'd have it amputated—on the spot!
FRIENDLY: How do you drink with such a nose?
You ought to have a cup made specially.
DESCRIPTIVE: 'Tis a rock—a crag—a cape—
A cape? say rather, a peninsula!
INQUISITIVE: What is that receptacle—
A razor-case or a portfolio?
KINDLY: Ah, do you love the little birds
So much that when they come and sing to you,

You give them this to perch on? INSOLENT:
Sir, when you smoke, the neighbors must suppose
Your chimney is on fire. CAUTIOUS: Take care—
A weight like that might make you topheavy.
THOUGHTFUL: Somebody fetch my parasol—
Those delicate colors fade so in the sun!
PEDANTIC: Does not Aristophanes
Mention a mythologic monster called
Hippocampelephantocamelos?
Surely we have here the original!
FAMILIAR: Well, old torchlight! Hang your hat
Over that chandelier—it hurts my eyes.
ELOQUENT: When it blows, the typhoon howls,
And the clouds darken. DRAMATIC: When it bleeds—
The Red Sea! ENTERPRISING: What a sign
For some perfumer! LYRIC: Hark—the horn
Of Roland calls to summon Charlemagne!—
SIMPLE: When do they unveil the monument?
RESPECTFUL: Sir, I recognize in you
A man of parts, a man of prominence—
RUSTIC: Hey? What? Call that a nose? Na, na—
I be no fool like what you think I be—
That there's a blue cucumber! MILITARY:
Point against cavalry! PRACTICAL: Why not
A lottery with this for the grand prize?
Or—parodying Faustus in the play—
"Was this the nose that launched a thousand ships
And burned the topless towers of Ilium?"
These, my dear sir, are things you might have said
Had you some tinge of letters, or of wit

To color your discourse. But wit,—not so,
You never had an atom—and of letters,
You need but three to write you down—an **Ass**.
Moreover,—if you had the invention, here
Before these folk to make a jest of me—
Be sure you would not then articulate
The twentieth part of half a syllable
Of the beginning! For I say these things
Lightly enough myself, about myself,
But I allow none else to utter them.

DE GUICHE
(Tries to lead away the amazed VALVERT.)
Vicomte—come.

VALVERT
(Choking)
Oh— These arrogant grand airs!—
A clown who—look at him—not even gloves!
No ribbons—no lace—no buckles on his shoes—

CYRANO
I carry my adornments on my soul.
I do not dress up like a popinjay;
But inwardly, I keep my daintiness.
I do not bear with me, by any chance,
An insult not yet washed away—a conscience
Yellow with unpurged bile—an honor frayed
To rags, a set of scruples badly worn.
I go caparisoned in gems unseen,
Trailing white plumes of freedom, garlanded
With my good name—no figure of a man,

But a soul clothed in shining armor, hung
With deeds for decorations, twirling—thus—
A bristling wit, and swinging at my side
Courage, and on the stones of this old town
Making the sharp truth ring, like golden spurs!

VALVERT

But—

CYRANO

But I have no gloves! A pity too!
I had one—the last one of an old pair—
And lost that. Very careless of me. Some
Gentleman offered me an impertinence.
I left it—in his face.

VALVERT

Dolt, bumpkin, fool,
Insolent puppy, jobbernowl!

CYRANO

(*Removes his hat and bows.*)
Ah, yes?

And I—Cyrano-Savinien-Hercule
De Bergerac!

VALVERT

(*Turns away.*)
Buffoon!

CYRANO

(*Cries out as if suddenly taken with a cramp.*)
Oh!

VALVERT

(Turns back.)

Well, what now?

CYRANO

(With grimaces of anguish)
I must do something to relieve these cramps—
This is what comes of lack of exercise—
Ah!—

VALVERT

What is all this?

CYRANO

My sword has gone to sleep!

VALVERT

(Draws)
So be it!

CYRANO

You shall die exquisitely.

VALVERT

(Contemptuously)
Poet!

CYRANO

Why, yes, a poet, if you will;
So while we fence, I'll make you a Ballade
Extempore.

VALVERT

A Ballade?

CYRANO

Yes. You know
What that is?

VALVERT

I—

CYRANO

The Ballade, sir, is formed
Of three stanzas of eight lines each—

VALVERT

Oh, come!

CYRANO

And a refrain of four.

VALVERT

You—

CYRANO

I'll compose
One, while I fight with you; and at the end
Of the last line—thrust home!

VALVERT

Will you?

CYRANO

I will.

(*Declaims*)
"*Ballade of the duel at the Hôtel de Bourgogne
Between de Bergerac and a Bœotian.*"

VALVERT

(*Sneering*)
What do you mean by that?

CYRANO

Oh, that? The title.

THE CROWD

(*Excited*)

Come on—

A circle—

Quiet—

Down in front!

(TABLEAU. *A ring of interested spectators in the
centre of the floor, the Marquis and the Officers
mingling with the citizens and common folk.
Pages swarming up on men's shoulders to see
better; the Ladies in the boxes standing and leaning over. To the right,* DE GUICHE *and his following; to the left,* LE BRET, CUIGY, RAGUENEAU,
and others of CYRANO'S *friends.*)

CYRANO

(*Closes his eyes for an instant.*)

Stop . . . Let me choose my rimes. . . . Now! Here we
   go—

(*He suits the action to the word, throughout the
following:*)

Lightly I toss my hat away,
   Languidly over my arm let fall
The cloak that covers my bright array—
   Then out swords, and to work withal!

   A Launcelot, in his Lady's hall . . .
A Spartacus, at the Hippodrome! . . .
   I dally awhile with you, dear jackal,
Then, as I end the refrain, thrust home.

(The swords cross—the fight is on.)

Where shall I skewer my peacock? . . . Nay,
  Better for you to have shunned this brawl!—
Here, in the heart, thro' your ribbons gay?
  —In the belly, under your silken shawl?
  Hark, how the steel rings musical!
Mark how my point floats, light as the foam,
  Ready to drive you back to the wall,
Then, as I end the refrain, thrust home!

Ho, for a rime! . . . You are white as whey—
  You break, you cower, you cringe, you . . . crawl!
Tac!—and I parry your last essay:
  So may the turn of a hand forestall
  Life with its honey, death with its gall;
So may the turn of my fancy roam
  Free, for a time, till the rimes recall,
Then, as I end the refrain, thrust home!

(He announces solemnly.)

REFRAIN

Prince! Pray God, that is Lord of all,
Pardon your soul, for your time has come!
  Beat—pass—fling you aslant, asprawl—
Then, as I end the refrain . . .

  (He lunges; VALVERT staggers back and falls into
    the arms of his friends. CYRANO recovers, and sa-
    lutes.)

—Thrust home!

(Shouts. Applause from the boxes. Flowers and handkerchiefs come fluttering down. The Officers surround CYRANO *and congratulate him.* RAGUENEAU *dances for joy.* LE BRET *is unable to conceal his enthusiasm. The friends of* VALVERT *hold him up and help him away.)*

THE CROWD

(In one long cry)

Ah-h!

A CAVALIER

Superb!

A WOMAN

Simply sweet!

RAGUENEAU

Magnelephant!

A MARQUIS

A novelty!

LE BRET

Bah!

THE CROWD

(Thronging around CYRANO)

Compliments—regards—

Bravo!—

A WOMAN'S VOICE

Why, he's a hero!

A MUSKETEER

(*Advances quickly to* CYRANO, *with outstretched hands.*)

Monsieur, will **you**
Permit me?—It was altogether fine!
I think I may appreciate these things—
Moreover, I have been stamping for pure joy!
(*He retires quickly.*)

CYRANO

(*To* CUIGY)
What was that gentleman's name?

CUIGY

Oh . . . D'Artagnan.

LE BRET

(*Takes* CYRANO's *arm.*)
Come here and tell me—

CYRANO

Let this crowd go first—

(*To* BELLEROSE)
May we stay?

BELLEROSE

(*With great respect*)
Certainly!
(*Cries and cat-calls off stage.*)

JODELET

(*Comes down from the door where he has been looking out.*)
Hark!— Montfleury—
They are hooting him.

BELLEROSE

(*Solemnly*)

Sic transit gloria!

(*Changes his tone and shouts to the porter and the lamplighter.*)

—Strike! . . . Close the house! . . . Leave the lights—
We rehearse
The new farce after dinner.

(JODELET *and* BELLEROSE *go out after elaborately saluting* CYRANO.)

THE PORTER

(*To* CYRANO)

You do not dine?

CYRANO

I?—No!

(THE PORTER *turns away.*)

LE BRET

Why not?

CYRANO

(*Haughtily*)

Because—

(*Changing his tone when he sees* THE PORTER *has gone.*)

Because I have
No money.

LE BRET

(*Gesture of tossing*)

But—the purse of gold?

CYRANO

Farewell,

Paternal pension!

LE BRET

So you have, until
The first of next month—?

CYRANO
Nothing.

LE BRET

What a fool!—

CYRANO

But—what a gesture!

THE ORANGE-GIRL
(*Behind her little counter; coughs.*)
Hem!
(CYRANO *and* LE BRET *look around; she advances timidly.*)

Pardon, Monsieur . . .
A man ought never to go hungry . . .
(*Indicating the sideboard*)

See,

I have everything here . . .
(*Eagerly*)

Please!—

CYRANO

(*Uncovers*)

My dear child,

I cannot bend this Gascon pride of mine

To accept such a kindness— Yet, for fear
That I may give you pain if I refuse,
I will take . . .
> (*He goes to the sideboard and makes his selec-
> tion.*)
>> Oh, not very much! A grape . . .
> (*She gives him the bunch; he removes a single
> grape.*)

One only! And a glass of water . . .
> (*She starts to pour wine into it; he stops her.*)
>> Clear!

And . . . half a macaroon!
> (*He gravely returns the other half.*)

LE BRET
>> Old idiot!

THE ORANGE-GIRL
Please!—Nothing more?

CYRANO
>> Why, yes— Your hand to kiss.
> (*He kisses the hand which she holds out, as he
> would the hand of a princess.*)

THE ORANGE-GIRL
Thank you, sir.
> (*She curtseys.*)
>> Good-night.
> (*She goes out.*)

CYRANO
>> Now, I am listening.

*(Plants himself before the sideboard and arranges
　thereon—)*

Dinner!—

(—the macaroon)

Drink!—

(—the glass of water)

Dessert!—

(—the grape.)

There—now I'll sit down.

(Seats himself.)

Lord, I was hungry! Abominably!

(Eating)

Well!

LE BRET

These fatheads with the bellicose grand airs
Will have you ruined if you listen to them;
Talk to a man of sense and hear how all
Your swagger impresses him.

CYRANO

(Finishes his macaroon.)

Enormously.

LE BRET

The Cardinal—

CYRANO

(Beaming)

Was he there?

LE BRET

He must have thought you—

CYRANO

Original.

LE BRET

Well, but—

CYRANO

He is himself
A playwright. He will not be too displeased
That I have closed another author's play.

LE BRET

But look at all the enemies you have made!

CYRANO

(*Begins on the grape.*)
How many—do you think?

LE BRET

Just forty-eight
Without the women.

CYRANO

Count them.

LE BRET

Montfleury,
Baro, de Guiche, the Vicomte, the Old Man,
All the Academy—

CYRANO

Enough! You make me
Happy!

LE BRET

But where is all this leading you?
What is your plan?

CYRANO

I have been wandering—
Wasting my force upon too many plans.
Now I have chosen one.

LE BRET

What one?

CYRANO

The simplest—
To make myself in all things admirable!

LE BRET

Hmph!—Well, then, the real reason why you hate
Montfleury— Come, the truth, now!

CYRANO

(*Rises*)

That Silenus,
Who cannot hold his belly in his arms,
Still dreams of being sweetly dangerous
Among the women—sighs and languishes,
Making sheeps' eyes out of his great frog's face—
I hate him ever since one day he dared
Smile upon—
Oh, my friend, I seemed to see
Over some flower a great snail crawling!

LE BRET

(*Amazed*)

How,
What? Is it possible?—

CYRANO

(With a bitter smile)

For me to love? . . .

(Changing his tone; seriously)

I love.

LE BRET

May I know? You have never said—

CYRANO

Whom I love? Think a moment. Think of me—
Me, whom the plainest woman would despise—
Me, with this nose of mine that marches on
Before me by a quarter of an hour!
Whom should I love? Why—of course—it must be
The woman in the world most beautiful.

LE BRET

Most beautiful?

CYRANO

In all this world—most sweet
Also; most wise; most witty, and most fair!

LE BRET

Who and what is this woman?

CYRANO

Dangerous
Mortally, without meaning; exquisite
Without imagining. Nature's own snare
To allure manhood. A white rose wherein
Love lies in ambush for his natural prey.
Who knows her smile has known a perfect thing.

She creates grace in her own image, brings
Heaven to earth in one movement of her hand—
Nor thou, O Venus! balancing thy shell
Over the Mediterranean blue, nor thou,
Diana! marching through broad, blossoming woods,
Art so divine as when she mounts her chair,
And goes abroad through Paris!

LE BRET

Oh, well—of course,
That makes everything clear!

CYRANO

Transparently.

LE BRET

Madeleine Robin—your cousin?

CYRANO

Yes; Roxane.

LE BRET

And why not? If you love her, tell her so!
You have covered yourself with glory in her eyes
This very day.

CYRANO

My old friend—look at me,
And tell me how much hope remains for me
With its protuberance! Oh, I have no more
Illusions! Now and then—bah! I may grow
Tender, walking alone in the blue cool
Of evening, through some garden fresh with flowers
After the benediction of the rain;

My poor big devil of a nose inhales
April . . . and so I follow with my eyes
Where some boy, with a girl upon his arm,
Passes a patch of silver . . . and I feel
Somehow, I wish I had a woman too,
Walking with little steps under the moon,
And holding my arm so, and smiling. Then
I dream—and I forget. . . .

                        And then I see
The shadow of my profile on the wall!

LE BRET

My friend! . . .

CYRANO

              My friend, I have my bitter days,
Knowing myself so ugly, so alone.
Sometimes—

LE BRET

You weep?

CYRANO

(*Quickly*)

                    Oh, not that ever! No,
That would be too grotesque—tears trickling down
All the long way along this nose of mine?
I will not so profane the dignity
Of sorrow. Never any tears for me!
Why, there is nothing more sublime than tears,
Nothing!—Shall I make them ridiculous
In my poor person?

LE BRET
Love's no more than chance!

CYRANO
(*Shakes his head.*)
No. I love Cleopatra; do I appear
Cæsar? I adore Beatrice; have I
The look of Dante?

LE BRET
But your wit—your courage—
Why, that poor child who offered you just now
Your dinner!—She—you saw with your own eyes,
Her eyes did not avoid you.

CYRANO
(*Thoughtful*)
That is true . . .

LE BRET
Well then! Roxane herself, watching your duel,
Paler than—

CYRANO
Pale?—

LE BRET
Her lips parted, her hand
Thus at her breast— I saw it! Speak to her
Speak, man!

CYRANO
Through my nose? She might laugh at me.
That is the one thing in this world I fear!

THE PORTER

(*Followed by* The Duenna, *approaches* CYRANO
    respectfully.)
A lady asking for Monsieur.

CYRANO
                    Mon dieu . . .
Her Duenna!—

THE DUENNA
    (*A sweeping curtsey*)
                Monsieur . . .
                            A message for you:
From our good cousin we desire to know
When and where we may see him privately.

CYRANO
    (*Amazed*)
To see me?

THE DUENNA
    (*An elaborate reverence*)
            To see you. We have certain things
To tell you.

CYRANO
        Certain—

THE DUENNA
            Things.

CYRANO
    (*Trembling*)
                    Mon dieu! . . .

THE DUENNA

We go

To-morrow, at the first flush of the dawn,
To hear Mass at St. Roch. Then afterwards,
Where can we meet and talk a little?

CYRANO
(*Catching* LE BRET's *arm*)

Where?..

I— Ah, mon dieu! . . . mon dieu! . . .

THE DUENNA

Well?

CYRANO

I am thinking . . .

THE DUENNA

And you think?

CYRANO

I . . . The shop of Ragueneau . . .
Ragueneau—pastrycook . . .

THE DUENNA

Who dwells?—

CYRANO

Mon dieu! . . .
Oh, yes . . . Ah, mon dieu! . . . Rue St.-Honoré.

THE DUENNA

We are agreed. Remember—seven o'clock.
(*Reverence*)
Until then—

CYRANO

I'll be there.
(*The Duenna goes out.*)

CYRANO

(*Falls into the arms of* LE BRET)
        Me . . . to see me! . . .

LE BRET

You are not quite so gloomy.

CYRANO

        After all,
She knows that I exist—no matter why!

LE BRET

So now, you are going to be happy.

CYRANO

        Now! . . .
     (*Beside himself*)
I—I am going to be a storm—a flame—
I need to fight whole armies all alone;
I have ten hearts; I have a hundred arms; I feel
Too strong to war with mortals—
     (*He shouts at the top of his voice.*)
        BRING ME GIANTS!
     (*A moment since, the shadows of the comedians
     have been visible moving and posturing upon
     the stage. The violins have taken their places.*)

A VOICE

     (*From the stage*)
Hey—pst—less noise! We are rehearsing here!

CYRANO

(Laughs)

We are going.

> *(He turns up stage. Through the street door enter* CUIGY, BRISSAILLE, *and a number of officers, supporting* LIGNIÈRE, *who is now thoroughly drunk.)*

CUIGY

Cyrano!

CYRANO

What is it?

CUIGY

Here—

Here's your stray lamb!

CYRANO

(Recognizes LIGNIÈRE.)

Lignière—What's wrong with him?

CUIGY

He wants you.

BRISSAILLE

He's afraid to go home.

CYRANO

Why?

LIGNIÈRE

> *(Showing a crumpled scrap of paper and speaking with the elaborate logic of profound intoxication.)*

This letter—hundred against one—that's me—
I'm the one—all because of little song—

Good song— Hundred men, waiting, understand?
Porte de Nesle—way home— Might be dangerous—
Would you permit me spend the night with you?

CYRANO

A hundred—is that all? You are going home!

LIGNIÈRE

(*Astonished*)
Why—

CYRANO

(*In a voice of thunder, indicating the lighted lantern which The Porter holds up curiously as he regards the scene.*)
Take that lantern!
(LIGNIÈRE *precipitately seizes the lantern.*)
Forward march! I say
I'll be the man to-night that sees you home.
(*To the officers*)
You others follow—I want an audience!

CUIGY

A hundred against one—

CYRANO

Those are the odds
To-night!
(*The Comedians in their costumes are descending from the stage and joining the group.*)

LE BRET

But why help this—

CYRANO

Growling!
There goes Le Bret

LE BRET

—This drunkard here?

CYRANO

(*His hand on* LE BRET'S *shoulder*)

Because this drunkard—
This tun of sack, this butt of Burgundy—
Once in his life has done one lovely thing:
After the Mass, according to the form,
He saw, one day, the lady of his heart
Take holy water for a blessing. So
This one, who shudders at a drop of rain,
This fellow here—runs headlong to the font
Bends down and drinks it dry!

A SOUBRETTE

A pretty thought!
I say that was

CYRANO

Ah, was it not?

THE SOUBRETTE

(*To the others*)

But why
Against one poor poet, a hundred men?

CYRANO

March!
(*To the officers*)

And you gentlemen, remember now,
No rescue— Let me fight alone.

A COMEDIENNE

(Jumps down from the stage.)
Come on!

I'm going to watch—

CYRANO

Come along!

ANOTHER COMEDIENNE

(Jumps down, speaks to a Comedian costumed as an old man.)
You, Cassandre?

CYRANO

Come all of you—the Doctor, Isabelle,
Léandre—the whole company—a swarm
Of murmuring, golden bees—we'll parody
Italian farce and Tragedy-of-Blood;
Ribbons for banners, masks for blazonry,
And tambourines to be our rolling drums!

ALL THE WOMEN

(Jumping for joy)
Bravo!—My hood— My cloak— Hurry!

JODELET

(Mock heroic)
Lead on!—

CYRANO

(To the violins)
You violins—play us an overture—

> (*The violins join the procession which is forming.
> The lighted candles are snatched from the stage
> and distributed; it becomes a torchlight pro-
> cession.*)

Bravo!—Officers— Ladies in costume—
And twenty paces in advance. . . .

> (*He takes his station as he speaks.*)

                              Myself,

Alone, with glory fluttering over me,
Alone as Lucifer at war with heaven!
Remember—no one lifts a hand to help—
Ready there? One . . . two . . . three! Porter, the
    doors! . . .

> (*The Porter flings wide the great doors. We see
> in the dim moonlight a corner of old Paris,
> purple and picturesque.*)

Look—Paris dreams—nocturnal, nebulous,
Under blue moonbeams hung from wall to wall—
Nature's own setting for the scene we play!—
Yonder, behind her veil of mist, the Seine,
Like a mysterious and magic mirror
Trembles—

              And you shall see what you shall see!

ALL

To the Porte de Nesle!

CYRANO

> (*Erect upon the threshold*)
>   To the Porte de Nesle!
> (*He turns back for a moment to the Soubrette*)

Did you not ask, my dear, why against one
Singer they send a hundred swords?
    (*Quietly, drawing his own sword*)
                                   Because
They know this one man for a friend of mine!
    (*He goes out. The procession follows:* LIGNIÈRE
      *zigzagging at its head, then, the Comediennes on
      the arms of the Officers, then the Comedians,
      leaping and dancing as they go. It vanishes into
      the night to the music of the violins, illuminated
      by the flickering glimmer of the candles.*)

(*Curtain*)

THE SECOND ACT

THE BAKERY OF THE POETS

THE SHOP OF RAGUENEAU, *Baker and Pastrycook: a spacious affair at the corner of the Rue St.-Honoré and the Rue de l'Arbre Sec. The street, seen vaguely through the glass panes in the door at the back, is grey in the first light of dawn.*

In the foreground, at the Left, a Counter is surmounted by a Canopy of wrought iron from which are hanging ducks, geese, and white peacocks. Great crockery jars hold bouquets of common flowers, yellow sunflowers in particular. On the same side farther back, a huge fireplace; in front of it, between great andirons, of which each one supports a little saucepan, roast fowls revolve and weep into their dripping-pans. To the Right at the First Entrance, a door. Beyond it, Second Entrance, a staircase leads up to a little dining-room under the eaves, its interior visible through open shutters. A table is set there and a tiny Flemish candlestick is lighted; there one may retire to eat and drink in private. A wooden gallery, extending from the head of the stairway, seems to lead to other little dining-rooms.

In the centre of the shop, an iron ring hangs by a rope over a pulley so that it can be raised or lowered; adorned with game of various kinds hung from it by hooks, it has the appearance of a sort of gastronomic chandelier.

In the shadow under the staircase, ovens are glowing.

The spits revolve; the copper pots and pans gleam ruddily. Pastries in pyramids. Hams hanging from the rafters. The morning baking is in progress: a bustle of tall cooks and timid scullions and scurrying apprentices; a blossoming of white caps adorned with cock's feathers or the wings of guinea fowl. On wicker trays or on great metal platters they bring in rows of pastries and fancy dishes of various kinds.

Tables are covered with trays of cakes and rolls; others with chairs placed about them are set for guests.

One little table in a corner disappears under a heap of papers. At the CURTAIN RISE RAGUENEAU *is seated there. He is writing poetry.*

A PASTRYCOOK

(*Brings in a dish.*)
Fruits *en gelée!*

SECOND PASTRYCOOK

(*Brings dish.*)
Custard!

THIRD PASTRYCOOK

(*Brings roast peacock ornamented with feathers.*)
Peacock *roti!*

FOURTH PASTRYCOOK

(*Brings tray of cakes.*)
Cakes and confections!

FIFTH PASTRYCOOK

(*Brings earthen dish.*)
Beef *en casserole!*

RAGUENEAU

(*Raises his head; returns to mere earth.*)
Over the coppers of my kitchen flows
The frost-silver dawn. Silence awhile
The god who sings within thee, Ragueneau!
Lay down the lute—the oven calls for thee!
(*Rises; goes to one of the cooks.*)
Here's a hiatus in your sauce; fill up
The measure.

THE COOK

How much?

RAGUENEAU

(*Measures on his finger.*)
One more dactyl.

THE COOK

Huh? ..

FIRST PASTRYCOOK

Rolls!

SECOND PASTRYCOOK

Roulades!

RAGUENEAU

(*Before the fireplace*)
Veil, O Muse, thy virgin eyes
From the lewd gleam of these terrestrial fires!
(*To First Pastrycook*)
Your rolls lack balance. Here's the proper form—
An equal hemistich on either side,
And the cæsura in between.
(*To another, pointing out an unfinished pie*)

                                Your house
Of crust should have a roof upon it.
        (*To another, who is seated on the hearth, placing
        poultry on a spit*)
                                            And you—

Along the interminable spit, arrange
The modest pullet and the lordly Turk
Alternately, my son—as great Malherbe
Alternates male and female rimes. Remember,
A couplet, or a roast, should be well turned.

                    AN APPRENTICE
        (*Advances with a dish covered by a napkin.*)
Master, I thought of you when I designed
This, hoping it might please you.

                    RAGUENEAU
                                    Ah! A Lyre—

                    THE APPRENTICE
In puff-paste—

                    RAGUENEAU
            And the jewels—candied fruit!

                    THE APPRENTICE
And the strings, barley-sugar!

                    RAGUENEAU
        (*Gives him money.*)
                            Go and drink
My health.
        (LISE *enters.*)

St!—My wife— Circulate, and hide
That money!
(Shows the Lyre to LISE, *with a languid air.)*
Graceful—yes?

LISE

Ridiculous!
(She places on the counter a pile of paper bags.)

RAGUENEAU

Paper bags? Thank you . . .
(He looks at them.)
Ciel! My manuscripts!
The sacred verses of my poets—rent
Asunder, limb from limb—butchered to make
Base packages of pastry! Ah, you are one
Of those insane Bacchantes who destroyed
Orpheus!

LISE

Your dirty poets left them here
To pay for eating half our stock-in-trade:
We ought to make some profit out of them!

RAGUENEAU

Ant! Would you blame the locust for his song?

LISE

I blame the locust for his appetite!
There used to be a time—before you had
Your hungry friends—you never called me Ants—
No, nor Bacchantes!

RAGUENEAU

What a way to use

Poetry!

LISE

Well, what is the use of it?

RAGUENEAU

But, my dear girl, what would you do with prose?
        (*Two Children enter.*)
Well, dears?

A CHILD

Three little patties.

RAGUENEAU

        (*Serves them.*)

There we are!

All hot and brown.

THE CHILD

Would you mind wrapping them?

RAGUENEAU

One of my paper bags! . . .

Oh, certainly..
        (*Reads from the bag, as he is about to wrap the
        patties in it.*)
"*Ulysses, when he left Penelope*"—
Not that one!
        (*Takes another bag; reads.*)
                "*Phœbus, golden-crowned*"—

Not that one.

LISE

Well? They are waiting!

RAGUENEAU

Very well, very well!—

The Sonnet to Phyllis . . .

Yet—it does seem hard . . .

LISE

Made up your mind—at last! Mph! Jack-o'-Dreams!

RAGUENEAU

(As her back is turned, calls back the Children, who are already at the door.)

Pst!—Children— Give me back the bag. Instead
Of three patties, you shall have six of them!

(Makes the exchange. The Children go out. He reads from the bag, as he smoothes it out tenderly.)

"Phyllis"—

A spot of butter on her name!—

"Phyllis"—

CYRANO

(Enters hurriedly.)

What is the time?

RAGUENEAU

Six o'Clock.

CYRANO

One

Hour more . . .

RAGUENEAU

Felicitations!

CYRANO

And for what?

RAGUENEAU

Your victory! I saw it all—

CYRANO

Which one?

RAGUENEAU

At the Hôtel de Bourgogne.

CYRANO

Oh—the duel!

RAGUENEAU

The duel in Rime!

LISE

He talks of nothing else.

CYRANO

Nonsense!

RAGUENEAU

(*Fencing and foining with a spit, which he snatches up from the hearth.*)
        "*Then, as I end the refrain, thrust home!*"
"*Then, as I end the refrain*"—

Gods! What a line!
"*Then, as I end*"—

CYRANO

What time now, Ragueneau?

RAGUENEAU

(*Petrified at the full extent of a lunge, while he looks at the clock.*)
Five after six—

(*Recovers*)
> "—thrust home!"

> A Ballade, too!

LISE

(*To* CYRANO, *who in passing has mechanically
  shaken hands with her*)
Your hand—what have you done?

CYRANO

> Oh, my hand?—Nothing

RAGUENEAU

What danger now—

CYRANO

> No danger.

LISE

> I believe

He is lying.

CYRANO

> Why? Was I looking down my nose!
That must have been a devil of a lie!
> (*Changing his tone; to* RAGUENEAU)
I expect someone. Leave us here alone,
When the time comes.

RAGUENEAU

> How can I? In a moment,
My poets will be here.

LISE

> To break their . . . fast!

CYRANO

Take them away, then, when I give the sign.
—What time?

RAGUENEAU

Ten minutes after.

CYRANO

Have you a pen?

RAGUENEAU

(*Offers him a pen.*)
An eagle's feather!

A MUSKETEER

(*Enters, and speaks to* LISE *in a stentorian voice.*)
Greeting!

CYRANO

(*To* RAGUENEAU)

Who is this?

RAGUENEAU

My wife's friend. A terrific warrior,
So he says.

CYRANO

Ah— I see.
(*Takes up the pen; waves* RAGUENEAU *away.*)
Only to write—
To fold— To give it to her—and to go . . .
(*Throws down the pen.*)
Coward! And yet—the Devil take my soul
If I dare speak one word to her . . .
(*To* RAGUENEAU)

What time now?

RAGUENEAU

A quarter after six.

CYRANO

(*Striking his breast*)
           —One little word
Of all the many thousand I have here!
Whereas in writing . . .
    (*Takes up the pen.*)
                Come, I'll write to her
That letter I have written on my heart,
Torn up, and written over many times—
So many times . . . that all I have to do
Is to remember, and to write it down.
    (*He writes. Through the glass of the door appear*
       vague and hesitating shadows. The Poets enter
       clothed in rusty black and spotted with mud.)

LISE

(*To* RAGUENEAU)
Here come your scarecrows!

FIRST POET

           Comrade!

SECOND POET

(*Takes both* RAGUENEAU's *hands.*)
               My dear brother!

THIRD POET

(*Sniffing*)
O Lord of Roasts, how sweet thy dwellings are!

FOURTH POET

Phoebus Apollo of the Silver Spoon!

FIFTH POET

Cupid of Cookery!

RAGUENEAU

(Surrounded, embraced, beaten on the back)
These geniuses,
They put one at one's ease!

FIRST POET

We were delayed
By the crowd at the Porte de Nesle.

SECOND POET

Dead men
All scarred and gory, scattered on the stones,
Villainous-looking scoundrels—eight of them.

CYRANO

(Looks up an instant.)
Eight? I thought only seven—

RAGUENEAU

Do you know
The hero of this hecatomb?

CYRANO

I? . . . No.

LISE

(To the Musketeer)
Do you?

THE MUSKETEER

Hmm—perhaps!

FIRST POET

They say one man alone
Put to flight all this crowd.

SECOND POET

Everywhere lay
Swords, daggers, pikes, bludgeons—

CYRANO

(*Writing*)

"*Your eyes . . .*"

THIRD POET

As fa

As the Quai des Orfevres, hats and cloaks—

FIRST POET

Why, that man must have been the devil!

CYRANO

"*Your lips . . .*"

FIRST POET

Some savage monster might have done this thing!

CYRANO

"*Looking upon you, I grow faint with fear . . .*"

SECOND POET

What have you written lately, Ragueneau?

CYRANO

"*Your Friend—"Who loves you . . .*"
So. No signature;
I'll give it to her myself.

RAGUENEAU
A Recipe
In Rime.

THIRD POET
Read us your rimes!

FOURTH POET
Here's a brioche
Cocking its hat at me.
  (*He bites off the top of it.*)

FIRST POET
Look how those buns
Follow the hungry poet with their eyes—
Those almond eyes!

SECOND POET
We are listening—

THIRD POET
See this cream-puff—
Fat little baby, drooling while it smiles!

SECOND POET
  (*Nibbling at the pastry Lyre.*)
For the first time, the Lyre is my support.

RAGUENEAU
  (*Coughs, adjusts his cap, strikes an attitude.*)
A Recipe in Rime—

SECOND POET
  (*Gives* FIRST POET *a dig with his elbow.*)
Your breakfast?

FIRST POET

Dinner!

RAGUENEAU

(*Declaims*)

A Recipe for Making Almond Tarts.

Beat your eggs, the yolk and white,
    Very light;
Mingle with their creamy fluff
  Drops of lime-juice, cool and green;
    Then pour in
Milk of Almonds, just enough.

Dainty patty-pans, embraced
    In puff-paste—
Have these ready within reach;
  With your thumb and finger, pinch
    Half an inch
Up around the edge of each—

Into these, a score or more,
    Slowly pour
All your store of custard; so
  Take them, bake them golden-brown—
    Now sit down! . . .
Almond tartlets, Ragueneau!

THE POETS

Delicious! Melting!

A POET

(Chokes)

Humph!

CYRANO

(To RAGUENEAU*)*

Do you not see
Those fellows fattening themselves?—

RAGUENEAU

I know.
I would not look—it might embarrass them—
You see, I love a friendly audience.
Besides—another vanity—I am pleased
When they enjoy my cooking.

CYRANO

(Slaps him on the back.)

Be off with you!—

*(*RAGUENEAU *goes up stage.)*
Good little soul!

(Calls to LISE.*)*

Madame!—

*(She leaves the Musketeer and comes down to
him.)*

This musketeer—
He is making love to you?

LISE

(Haughtily)

If any man
Offends my virtue—all I have to do
Is look at him—once!

CYRANO

(*Looks at her gravely; she drops her eyes.*)
I do not find
Those eyes of yours unconquerable.

LISE

(*Panting*)

—Ah!

CYRANO

(*Raising his voice a little*)
Now listen— I am fond of Ragueneau;
I allow no one—do you understand?—
To . . . take his name in vain!

LISE

You think—

CYRANO

(*Ironic emphasis*)

I think
I interrupt you.
(*He salutes the Musketeer, who has heard without
daring to resent the warning. LISE goes to the
Musketeer as he returns CYRANO's salute.*)

LISE

You—you swallow that?—
You ought to have pulled his nose!

THE MUSKETEER

His nose?—His nose! . . .
(*He goes out hurriedly. ROXANE and the Duenna
appear outside the door.*)

CYRANO

(*Nods to* RAGUENEAU.)

Pst!—

RAGUENEAU

(*To the Poets*)

Come inside—

CYRANO

(*Impatient*)

Pst! . . . Pst! . . .

RAGUENEAU

We shall be more

Comfortable . . .

(*He leads The Poets into inner room.*)

FIRST POET

The cakes!

SECOND POET

Bring them along!

(*They go out.*)

CYRANO

If I can see the faintest spark of hope,
Then—

(*Throws door open—bows.*)

Welcome!

(ROXANE *enters, followed by the Duenna, whom* CYRANO *detains.*)

Pardon me—one word—

THE DUENNA

Take two.

CYRANO

Have you a good digestion ?

THE DUENNA

Wonderful!

CYRANO

Good. Here are two sonnets, by Benserade—

THE DUENNA

Euh?

CYRANO

Which I fill for you with éclairs.

THE DUENNA

Ooo!

CYRANO

Do you like cream-puffs?

THE DUENNA

Only with whipped cream.

CYRANO

Here are three . . . six—embosomed in a poem
By Saint-Amant. This ode of Chapelin
Looks deep enough to hold—a jelly roll.
—Lo you love Nature?

THE DUENNA

Mad about it.

CYRANO

Then

Go out and eat these in the street. Do not
Return—

THE DUENNA

Oh, but—

CYRANO

Until you finish them.

(*Down to* ROXANE)

Blessed above all others be the hour
When you remembered to remember me,
And came to tell me . . . what?

ROXANE

(*Takes off her mask.*)

First let me thank you
Because . . . That man . . . that creature, whom your
    sword
Made sport of yesterday— His patron, one—

CYRANO

De Guiche?—

ROXANE

—who thinks himself in love with me
Would have forced that man upon me for—
    a husband—

CYRANO

I understand—so much the better then!
I fought, not for my nose, but your bright eyes.

ROXANE

And then, to tell you—but before I can
Tell you— Are you, I wonder, still the same
Big brother—almost—that you used to be
When we were children, playing by the pond
In the old garden down there—

CYRANO

I remember—
Every summer you came to Bergerac! . . .

ROXANE

You used to make swords out of bulrushes—

CYRANO

You dandelion-dolls with golden hair—

ROXANE

And those green plums—

CYRANO

And those black mulberries—

ROXANE

In those days, you did everything I wished!

CYRANO

Roxane, in short skirts, was called Madeleine.

ROXANE

Was I pretty?

CYRANO

Oh—not too plain!

ROXANE

Sometimes
When you had hurt your hand you used to come
Running to me—and I would be your mother,
And say— Oh, in a very grown-up voice:
    (*She takes his hand.*)
"*Now,* what have you been doing to yourself?
Let me see—"
    (*She sees the hand—starts.*)

Oh!—

Wait—I said *Let me see!*
Still—at your age! How did you do that?

CYRANO

Playing
With the big boys, down by the Porte de Nesle.

ROXANE

(*Sits at a table and wets her handkerchief in a
    glass of water.*)
Come here to me.

CYRANO

—Such a wise little mother!

ROXANE

And tell me, while I wash this blood away,
How many you—played with?

CYRANO

Oh, about a hundred.

ROXANE

Tell me.

CYRANO

No. Let me go. Tell me what *you*
Were going to tell *me*—if you dared?

ROXANE

(*Still holding his hand*)

I think
I do dare—now. It seems like long ago
When I could tell you things. Yes—I dare . . .

Listen:
I . . . love someone.

CYRANO
Ah! . . .

ROXANE
Someone who does not know.

CYRANO
Ah! . . .

ROXANE
At least—not yet.

CYRANO
Ah! . . .

ROXANE
But he will know
Some day.

CYRANO
Ah! . . .

ROXANE
A big boy who loves me too,
And is afraid of me, and keeps away,
And never says one word.

CYRANO
Ah! . . .

ROXANE
Let me have
Your hand a moment—why, how hot it is!—
I know. I see him trying . . .

CYRANO

Ah! . . .

ROXANE

There now!

Is that better?—

(*She finishes bandaging the hand with her handkerchief.*)

Besides—only to think—

(This is a secret.) He is a soldier too,
In your own regiment—

CYRANO

Ah! . . .

ROXANE

Yes, in the Guards.

Your company too.

CYRANO

Ah! . . .

ROXANE

And such a man!—

He is proud—noble—young—brave—beautiful—

CYRANO

(*Turns pale; rises.*)

Beautiful!—

ROXANE

What's the matter?

CYRANO

(*Smiling*)

Nothing—this—

My sore hand!

ROXANE

Well, I love him. That is all.
Oh—and I never saw him anywhere
Except the *Comédie*.

CYRANO

You have never spoken?—

ROXANE

Only our eyes . . .

CYRANO

Why, then— How do you know?—

ROXANE

People talk about people; and I hear
Things . . . and I know.

CYRANO

You say he is in the Guards:
His name?

ROXANE

Baron Christian de Neuvillette.

CYRANO

He is not in the Guards.

ROXANE

Yes. Since this morning.
Captain Carbon de Castel-Jaloux.

CYRANO

So soon! . . .
So soon we lose our hearts!—
But, my dear child,—

THE DUENNA

(Opens the door.)

I have eaten the cakes, Monsieur de Bergerac!

CYRANO

Good! Now go out and read the poetry!
(The Duenna disappears.)
—But, my dear child! You, who love only words,
Wit, the grand manner— Why, for all you know,
The man may be a savage, or a fool.

ROXANE

His curls are like a hero from D'Urfé.

CYRANO

His mind may be as curly as his hair.

ROXANE

Not with such eyes. I read his soul in them.

CYRANO

Yes, all our souls are written in our eyes!
But—if he be a bungler?

ROXANE

                    Then I shall die—
There!

CYRANO

(After a pause)
                    And you brought me here to tell me this?
I do not yet quite understand, Madame,
The reason for your confidence.

ROXANE

                    They say

That in your company— It frightens me—
You are all Gascons . . .

CYRANO

And we pick a quarrel
With any flat-foot who intrudes himself,
Whose blood is not pure Gascon like our own?
Is this what you have heard?

ROXANE

I am so afraid
For him!

CYRANO

(*Between his teeth*)
Not without reason!—

ROXANE

And I thought
You . . . You were so brave, so invincible
Yesterday, against all those brutes!—If you,
Whom they all fear—

CYRANO

Oh, well—I will defend
Your little Baron.

ROXANE

Will you? Just for me?
Because I have always been—your friend!

CYRANO

Of course . . .

ROXANE

Will you be *his* friend?

CYRANO

I will be his friend.

ROXANE

And never let him fight a duel?

CYRANO

No—never.

ROXANE

Oh, but you are a darling!—I must go—
You never told me about last night— Why,
You must have been a hero! Have him write
And tell me all about it—will you?

CYRANO

Of course . . .

ROXANE

(*Kisses her hand.*)
I always did love you!—A hundred men
Against one— Well. . . . Adieu. We are great friends,
Are we not?

CYRANO

Of course . . .

ROXANE

He *must* write to me—
A hundred— You shall tell me the whole story
Some day, when I have time. A hundred men—
What courage!

CYRANO

(*Salutes as she goes out.*)
Oh . . . I have done better since!

(The door closes after her. CYRANO *remains motion-less, his eyes on the ground. Pause. The other door opens;* RAGUENEAU *puts in his head.)*

RAGUENEAU

May I come in?

CYRANO

(Without moving)
Yes . . .
*(*RAGUENEAU *and his friends re-enter. At the same time,* CARBON DE CASTEL-JALOUX *appears at the street door in uniform as Captain of the Guards; recognizes* CYRANO *with a sweeping gesture.)*

CARBON

Here he is!—Our hero!

CYRANO

(Raises his head and salutes.)
Our Captain!

CARBON

We know! All our company
Are here—

CYRANO

(Recoils)
No—

CARBON

Come! They are waiting for you.

CYRANO

No!

CARBON

(*Tries to lead him out.*)
Only across the street— Come!

CYRANO

Please—

CARBON

(*Goes to the door and shouts in a voice of thunder.*)
Our champion

Refuses! He is not feeling well to-day!

A VOICE OUTSIDE

Ah! Sandious!
(*Noise outside of swords and trampling feet approaching.*)

CARBON

Here they come now!

THE CADETS

(*Entering the shop*)

Mille dious!—

Mordious!—Capdedious!—Pocapdedious!

RAGUENEAU

(*In astonishment*)

Gentlemen—

You are all Gascons?

THE CADETS
All!

FIRST CADET

(*To* CYRANO)

Bravo!

CYRANO

Baron!

ANOTHER CADET
(Takes both his hands.)
Vivat!

CYRANO

Baron!

THIRD CADET
Come to my arms!

CYRANO

Baron!

OTHERS
To mine!—To mine!—

CYRANO
Baron . . . Baron . . . Have mercy—

RAGUENEAU
You are all Barons too?

THE CADETS
Are we?

RAGUENEAU

Are they? . . .

FIRST CADET
Our coronets would star the midnight sky!

LE BRET
(Enters; hurries to CYRANO.*)*
The whole Town's looking for you! Raving mad—
A triumph! Those who saw the fight—

CYRANO

I hope

You have not told them where I—

LE BRET

(*Rubbing his hand*)

Certainly

I told them!

CITIZEN

(*Enters, followed by a group.*)

Listen! Shut the door!—Here comes

All Paris!

(*The street outside fills with a shouting crowd.
Chairs and carriages stop at the door.*)

LE BRET

(*Aside to* CYRANO, *smiling*)

And Roxane?

CYRANO

(*Quickly*)

Hush!

THE CROWD OUTSIDE

Cyrano!

(*A mob bursts into the shop. Shouts, acclamations,
general disturbance.*)

RAGUENEAU

(*Standing on a table*)

My shop invaded— They'll break everything—
Glorious!

SEVERAL MEN

(Crowding about CYRANO)
My friend . . . My friend! . . .

CYRANO

Why, yesterday
I did not have so many friends!

LE BRET

Success
At last!

A MARQUIS

(Runs to CYRANO, *with outstretched hands.)*
My dear—really!—

CYRANO

(Coldly)

So? And how long
Have I been dear to you?

ANOTHER MARQUIS

One moment—pray!
I have two ladies in my carriage here;
Let me present you—

CYRANO

Certainly! And first,
Who will present you, sir,—to me?

LE BRET

(Astounded)

Why, what
The devil?—

CYRANO

Hush!

A MAN OF LETTERS
(*With a portfolio*)

May I have the details? . . .

CYRANO

You may not.

LE BRET
(*Plucking* CYRANO's *sleeve*)

Theophraste Renaudot!—Editor
Of the *Gazette*—your reputation! . . .

CYRANO

No!

A POET

(*Advances*)
Monsieur—

CYRANO

Well?

THE POET

Your full name? I will compose
A pentacrostic—

ANOTHER

Monsieur—

CYRANO

That will do!
(*Movement. The crowd arranges itself.* DE GUICHE
appears, escorted by CUIGY, BRISSAILLE, *and the*

other officers who were with CYRANO *at the close of the First Act.*)

CUIGY

(*Goes to* CYRANO.)
Monsieur de Guiche!—
(*Murmur. Everyone moves.*)
A message from the Marshal

De Gassion—

DE GUICHE

(*Saluting* CYRANO)
Who wishes to express
Through me his admiration. He has heard
Of your affair—

THE CROWD

Bravo!

CYRANO

(*Bowing*)
The Marshal speaks
As an authority.

DE GUICHE

He said just now
The story would have been incredible
Were it not for the witness—

CUIGY

Of our eyes!

LE BRET

(*Aside to* CYRANO)
What is it?

CYRANO

Hush!—

LE BRET

Something is wrong with you;
Are you in pain?

CYRANO

(*Recovering himself*)
In pain? Before this crowd?
(*His moustache bristles. He throws out his chest.*)
I? In pain? You shall see!

DE GUICHE

(*To whom* CUIGY *has been whispering.*)
Your name is known
Already as a soldier. You are one
Of those wild Gascons, are you not?

CYRANO

The Guards,
Yes. A Cadet.

A CADET

(*In a voice of thunder*)
One of ourselves!

DE GUICHE

Ah! So
Then all these gentlemen with the haughty air,
These are the famous—

CARBON

Cyrano!

CYRANO

Captain?

CARBON

Our troop being all present, be so kind
As to present them to the Comte de Guiche!

CYRANO

(*With a gesture presenting the Cadets to* DE
GUICHE, *declaims:*)

The Cadets of Gascoyne—the defenders
  Of Carbon de Castel-Jaloux:
Free fighters, free lovers, free spenders—
The Cadets of Gascoyne—the defenders
Of old homes, old names, and old splendors—
  A proud and a pestilent crew!
The Cadets of Gascoyne, the defenders
  Of Carbon de Castel-Jaloux.

Hawk-eyed, they stare down all contenders—
  The wolf bares his fangs as they do—
Make way there, you fat money-lenders!
(Hawk-eyed, they stare down all contenders)
Old boots that have been to the menders,
  Old cloaks that are worn through and through—
Hawk-eyed, they stare down all contenders—
  The wolf bares his fangs as they do!

Skull-breakers they are, and sword-benders;
  Red blood is their favorite brew;
Hot haters and loyal befrienders,
Skull-breakers they are, and sword-benders.

Wherever a quarrel engenders,
They're ready and waiting for you!
Skull-breakers they are, and sword-benders;
Red blood is their favorite brew!

Behold them, our Gascon defenders
Who win every woman they woo!
There's never a dame but surrenders—
Behold them, our Gascon defenders!
Young wives who are clever pretenders—
Old husbands who house the cuckoo—
Behold them—our Gascon defenders
Who win every woman they woo!

DE GUICHE

(*Languidly, sitting in a chair*)

Poets are fashionable nowadays
To have about one. Would you care to join
My following?

CYRANO

No, sir. I do not follow.

DE GUICHE

Your duel yesterday amused my uncle
The Cardinal. I might help you there.

LE BRET

Grand Dieu!

DE GUICHE

I suppose you have written a tragedy—
They all have.

LE BRET

(*Aside to* CYRANO)

    Now at last you'll have it played—
Your *Agrippine!*

DE GUICHE

Why not? Take it to him.

CYRANO

(*Tempted*)
Really—

DE GUICHE

He is himself a dramatist;
Let him rewrite a few lines here and there,
And he'll approve the rest.

CYRANO

(*His face falls again.*)
     Impossible.
My blood curdles to think of altering
One comma.

DE GUICHE

    Ah, but when he likes a thing
He pays well.

CYRANO

    Yes—but not so well as I—
When I have made a line that sings itself
So that I love the sound of it—I pay
Myself a hundred times.

DE GUICHE

    You are proud, my friend.

CYRANO

You have observed that?

A CADET

(*Enters with a drawn sword, along the whole blade
of which is transfixed a collection of disreputable
hats, their plumes draggled, their crowns cut and
torn.*)

Cyrano! See here—
Look what we found this morning in the street—
The plumes dropped in their flight by those fine birds
Who showed the white feather!

CARBON

Spoils of the hunt—
Well mounted!

THE CROWD
Ha-ha-ha!

CUIGY

Whoever hired
Those rascals, he must be an angry man
To-day!

BRISSAILLE
Who was it? Do you know?

DE GUICHE

Myself!—

(*The laughter ceases.*)
I hired them to do the sort of work
We do not soil our hands with—punishing
A drunken poet. . . .

(*Uncomfortable silence*)

THE CADET

(*To* CYRANO)

What shall we do with them?
They ought to be preserved before they spoil—

CYRANO

(*Takes the sword, and in the gesture of saluting* DE
GUICHE *with it, makes all the hats slide off at
his feet.*)

Sir, will you not return these to your friends?

DE GUICHE

My chair—my porters here—immediately!
(*To* CYRANO *violently*)
—As for you, sir!—

A VOICE

(*In the street*)

The chair of Monseigneur
Le Comte de Guiche!—

DE GUICHE

(*Who has recovered his self-control; smiling*)
Have you read *Don Quixote?*

CYRANO

I have—and found myself the hero.

A PORTER

(*Appears at the door.*)

Chair
Ready!

DE GUICHE

Be so good as to read once more
The chapter of the windmills.

CYRANO

(*Gravely*)

Chapter Thirteen.

DE GUICHE

Windmills, remember, if you fight with them—

CYRANO

My enemies change, then, with every wind?

DE GUICHE

—May swing round their huge arms and cast you down
Into the mire.

CYRANO

Or up—among the stars!

(De Guiche *goes out. We see him get into the
chair. The Officers follow murmuring among
themselves.* Le Bret *goes up with them. The
crowd goes out.*)

CYRANO

(*Saluting with burlesque politeness, those who go
out without daring to take leave of him.*)

Gentlemen. . . . Gentlemen. . . .

LE BRET

(*As the door closes, comes down, shaking his
clenched hands to heaven.*)

You have done it now—
You have made your fortune!

CYRANO

There you go again,

Growling!—

LE BRET

At least this latest pose of yours—
Ruining every chance that comes your way—
Becomes exaggerated—

CYRANO

Very well,

Then I exaggerate!

LE BRET

(*Triumphantly*)

Oh, you do!

CYRANO

Yes;

On principle. There are things in this world
A man does well to carry to extremes.

LE BRET

Stop trying to be Three Musketeers in one!
Fortune and glory—

CYRANO

What would you have me do?
Seek for the patronage of some great man,
And like a creeping vine on a tall tree
Crawl upward, where I cannot stand alone?
No, thank you! Dedicate, as others do,
Poems to pawnbrokers? Be a buffoon
In the vile hope of teasing out a smile
On some cold face? No, thank you! Eat a toad
For breakfast every morning? Make my knees
Callous, and cultivate a supple spine,—

Wear out my belly grovelling in the dust?
No, thank you! Scratch the back of any swine
That roots up gold for me? Tickle the horns
Of Mammon with my left hand, while my right
Too proud to know his partner's business,
Takes in the fee? No, thank you! Use the fire
God gave me to burn incense all day long
Under the nose of wood and stone? No, thank you!
Shall I go leaping into ladies' laps
And licking fingers?—or—to change the form—
Navigating with madrigals for oars,
My sails full of the sighs of dowagers?
No thank you! Publish verses at my own
Expense? No, thank you! Be the patron saint
Of a small group of literary souls
Who dine together every Tuesday? No
I thank you! Shall I labor night and day
To build a reputation on one song,
And never write another? Shall I find
True genius only among Geniuses,
Palpitate over little paragraphs,
And struggle to insinuate my name
Into the columns of the *Mercury*?
No, thank you! Calculate, scheme, be afraid,
Love more to make a visit than a poem,
Seek introductions, favors, influences?—
No, thank you! No, I thank you! And again
I thank you!—But . . .

               To sing, to laugh, to dream,
To walk in my own way and be alone,

Free, with an eye to see things as they are,
A voice that means manhood—to cock my hat
Where I choose—At a word, a *Yes,* a *No,*
To fight—or write. To travel any road
Under the sun, under the stars, nor doubt
If fame or fortune lie beyond the bourne—
Never to make a line I have not heard
In my own heart; yet, with all modesty
To say: "My soul, be satisfied with flowers,
With fruit, with weeds even; but gather them
In the one garden you may call your own."
So, when I win some triumph, by some chance,
Render no share to Cæsar—in a word,
I am too proud to be a parasite,
And if my nature wants the germ that grows
Towering to heaven like the mountain pine,
Or like the oak, sheltering multitudes—
I stand, not high it may be—but alone!

LE BRET

Alone, yes!—but why stand against the world?
What devil has possessed you now, to go
Everywhere making yourself enemies?

CYRANO

Watching you other people making friends
Everywhere—as a dog makes friends! I mark
The manner of these canine courtesies
And think: "My friends are of a cleaner breed;
Here comes—thank God!—another enemy!"

LE BRET

But this is madness!

CYRANO
                    Method, let us say.
It is my pleasure to displease. I love
Hatred. Imagine how it feels to face
The volley of a thousand angry eyes—
The bile of envy and the froth of fear
Spattering little drops about me— You—
Good nature all around you, soft and warm—
You are like those Italians, in great cowls
Comfortable and loose— Your chin sinks down
Into the folds, your shoulders droop. But I—
The Spanish ruff I wear around my throat
Is like a ring of enemies; hard, proud,
Each point another pride, another thorn—
So that I hold myself erect perforce,
Wearing the hatred of the common herd
Haughtily, the harsh collar of Old Spain,
At once a fetter and—a halo!

LE BRET
                    Yes . . .
        (*After a silence, draws* CRYANO's *arm through his
          own.*)
Tell this to all the world— And then to me
Say very softly that . . . She loves you not.

CYRANO
        (*Quickly*)
Hush!

(A moment since, CHRISTIAN *has entered and mingled with the Cadets, who do not offer to speak to him. Finally, he sits down alone at a small table, where he is served by* LISE.*)*

A CADET

(Rises from a table up stage, his glass in his hand.)
Cyrano!—Your story!

CYRANO

Presently . . .
(He goes up, on the arm of LE BRET, *talking to him. The Cadets come down stage.)*

THE CADET

The story of the combat! An example
For—
(He stops by the table where CHRISTIAN *is sitting.)*
—this young tadpole here.

CHRISTIAN

(Looks up)

Tadpole?

ANOTHER CADET

Yes, you!—
You narrow-gutted Northerner!

CHRISTIAN

Sir?

FIRST CADET

Hark ye,
Monsieur de Neuvillette: You are to know

There is a certain subject—I would say,
A certain object—never to be named
Among us: utterly unmentionable!

CHRISTIAN

And that is?

THIRD CADET

(*In an awful voice*)
                Look at me! . . .
(*He strikes his nose three times with his finger,
    mysteriously.*)
                                You understand?

CHRISTIAN

Why, yes; the—

FOURTH CADET

                Sh! . . . We never speak that word—
(*Indicating* CYRANO *by a gesture*)
To breathe it is to have to do with HIM!

FIFTH CADET

(*Speaks through his nose.*)
He has exterminated several
Whose tone of voice suggested . . .

SIXTH CADET

(*In a hollow tone; rising from under the table on
    all fours.*)
                                Would you die
Before your time? Just mention anything
Convex . . . or cartilaginous . . .

SEVENTH CADET

(*His hand on* CHRISTIAN's *shoulder*)
                                        One word—
One syllable—one gesture—nay, one sneeze—
Your handkerchief becomes your winding-sheet!
        (*Silence. In a circle around* CHRISTIAN, *arms crossed,
        they regard him expectantly.*)

CHRISTIAN

(*Rises and goes to* CARBON, *who is conversing with
an officer, and pretending not to see what is taking place.*)
Captain!

CARBON

(*Turns, and looks him over.*)
        Sir?

CHRISTIAN

                    What is the proper thing to do
When Gascons grow too boastful?

CARBON

                                Prove to them
That one may be a Norman, and have courage.
        (*Turns his back.*)

CHRISTIAN

I thank you.

FIRST CADET

(*To* CYRANO)
        Come—the story!

ALL

The story!

CYRANO

(Comes down.)

Oh,

My story? Well . . .

(They all draw up their stools and group themselves
around him, eagerly. CHRISTIAN *places himself*
astride of a chair, his arms on the back of it.)

I marched on, all alone
To meet those devils. Overhead, the moon
Hung like a gold watch at the fob of heaven,
Till suddenly some Angel rubbed a cloud,
As it might be his handkerchief, across
The shining crystal, and—the night came down.
No lamps in those back streets— It was so dark—
Mordious! You could not see beyond—

CHRISTIAN

Your nose.

(Silence. Every man slowly rises to his feet. They
look at CYRANO *almost with terror. He has*
stopped short, utterly astonished. Pause.)

CYRANO

Who is that man there?

A CADET

(In a low voice)

A recruit—arrived

This morning.

CYRANO

(*Takes a step toward* CHRISTIAN)
A recruit—

CARBON

(*In a low voice*)

His name is Christian

De Neuvil—

CYRANO

(*Suddenly motionless*)
Oh . . .
(*He turns pale, flushes, makes a movement as if to
throw himself upon* CHRISTIAN.)
I—
(*Controls himself, and goes on in a choking voice.*)
I see. Very well,

As I was saying—
(*With a sudden burst of rage*)
Mordious! . . .
(*He goes on in a natural tone.*)
It grew dark,

You could not see your hand before your eyes.
I marched on, thinking how, all for the sake
Of one old souse
(*They slowly sit down, watching him.*)
who wrote a bawdy song

Whenever he took—

CHRISTIAN

A noseful—
(*Everyone rises.* CHRISTIAN *balances himself on two
legs of his chair.*)

CYRANO

(*Half strangled*)

—Took a notion . . .
Whenever he took a notion— For his sake,
I might antagonize some dangerous man,
One powerful enough to make me pay—

CHRISTIAN

Through the nose—

CYRANO

(*Wipes the sweat from his forehead.*)
—Pay the Piper. After all,
I thought, why am I putting in my—

CHRISTIAN

Nose—

CYRANO

—My oar . . . Why am I putting in my oar?
The quarrel's none of mine. However—now
I am here, I may as well go through with it.
Come, Gascon—do your duty!—Suddenly
A sword flashed in the dark. I caught it fair—

CHRISTIAN

On the nose—

CYRANO

On my blade. Before I knew it,
There I was—

CHRISTIAN

Rubbing noses—

CYRANO

(*Pale and smiling*)

Crossing swords

With half a score at once. I handed one—

CHRISTIAN

A nosegay—

CYRANO

(*Leaping at him*)
Ventre-Saint-Gris! . . .
(*The Gascons tumble over each other to get a good
view. Arrived in front of* CHRISTIAN, *who has not
moved an inch,* CYRANO *masters himself again,
and continues.*)

He went down;
The rest gave way; I charged—

CHRISTIAN

Nose in the air—

CYRANO

I skewered two of them—disarmed a third—
Another lunged— Paf! And I countered—

CHRISTIAN

Pif!

CYRANO

(*Bellowing*)
TONNERRE! Out of here—All of you!
(*All the Cadets rush for the door.*)

FIRST CADET

At last—

The old lion wakes!

CYRANO

All of you! Leave me here

Alone with that man!

(*The lines following are heard brokenly, in the confusion of getting through the door.*)

SECOND CADET

Bigre! He'll have the fellow

Chopped into sausage—

RAGUENEAU

Sausage?—

THIRD CADET

Mince-meat, then—

One of your pies!—

RAGUENEAU

Am I pale? You look white

As a fresh napkin—

CARBON

(*At the door*)

Come!

FOURTH CADET

He'll never leave

Enough of him to—

FIFTH CADET

Why, it frightens ME

To think of what will—

SIXTH CADET

(*Closing the door*)

Something horrible

Beyond imagination . . .

*(They are all gone: some through the street door,
some by the inner doors to right and left. A few
disappear up the staircase. CYRANO and CHRIS-
TIAN stand face to face a moment, and look at
each other.)*

CYRANO

To my arms!

CHRISTIAN

Sir? . . .

CYRANO

You have courage!

CHRISTIAN

Oh, that! . . .

CYRANO

You are brave—

That pleases me.

CHRISTIAN

You mean? . . .

CYRANO

Do you not know

I am her brother? Come!

CHRISTIAN

Whose?—

CYRANO

Hers—Roxane!

CHRISTIAN

Her . . . brother? You?
(*Hurries to him.*)

CYRANO

Her cousin. Much the same.

CHRISTIAN

And she has told you? . . .

CYRANO

Everything.

CHRISTIAN

She loves me?

CYRANO

Perhaps.

CHRISTIAN

(*Takes both his hands.*)
My dear sir—more than I can say,
I am honored—

CYRANO

This is rather sudden.

CHRISTIAN

Please
Forgive me—

CYRANO

(*Holds him at arm's length, looking at him.*)
Why, he is a handsome devil,
This fellow!

CHRISTIAN

On my honor—if you knew
How much I have admired—

CYRANO

Yes, yes—and all
Those Noses which—

CHRISTIAN

Please! I apologize.

CYRANO

(*Change of tone*)
Roxane expects a letter—

CHRISTIAN

Not from me?—

CYRANO

Yes. Why not?

CHRISTIAN

Once I write, that ruins all!

CYRANO

And why?

CHRISTIAN

Because . . . because I am a fool!
Stupid enough to hang myself!

CYRANO

But no—
You are no fool; you call yourself a fool,
There's proof enough in that. Besides, you did **not**
Attack me like a fool.

CHRISTIAN

Bah! Anyone
Can pick a quarrel. Yes, I have a sort
Of rough and ready soldier's tongue. I know
That. But with any woman—paralyzed,
Speechless, dumb. I can only look at them.
Yet sometimes, when I go away, their eyes . . .

CYRANO

Why not their hearts, if you should wait and see?

CHRISTIAN

No. I am one of those— I know—those men
Who never can make love.

CYRANO

                    Strange. . . . Now it seems
I, if I gave my mind to it, I might
Perhaps make love well.

CHRISTIAN

                    Oh, if I had words
To say what I have here!

CYRANO

                    If I could be
A handsome little Musketeer with eyes!—

CHRISTIAN

Besides—you know Roxane—how sensitive—
One rough word, and the sweet illusion—gone!

CYRANO

I wish you might be my interpreter.

CHRISTIAN

I wish I had your wit—

CYRANO

Borrow it, then!—
Your beautiful young manhood—lend me that,
And we two make one hero of romance!

CHRISTIAN

What?

CYRANO

Would you dare repeat to her the words
I gave you, day by day?

CHRISTIAN

You mean?

CYRANO

I mean
Roxane shall have no disillusionment!
Come, shall we win her both together? Take
The soul within this leathern jack of mine,
And breathe it into you?
(Touches him on the breast.)
So—there's my heart
Under your velvet, now!

CHRISTIAN

But— Cyrano!—

CYRANO

But— Christian, why not?

CHRISTIAN

I am afraid—

CYRANO

I know—

Afraid that when you have her all alone,
You lose all. Have no fear. It is yourself
She loves—give her yourself put into words—
My words, upon your lips!

CHRISTIAN

But . . . but your eyes! . . .

They burn like—

CYRANO

Will you? . . . Will you?

CHRISTIAN

Does it mean

So much to you?

CYRANO

(*Beside himself*)
It means—
(*Recovers, changes tone.*)
A Comedy,

A situation for a poet! Come,
Shall we collaborate? I'll be your cloak
Of darkness, your enchanted sword, your ring
To charm the fairy Princess!

CHRISTIAN

But the letter—

I cannot write—

CYRANO

Oh, yes, the letter.

(He takes from his pocket the letter which he has written.)

Here.

CHRISTIAN

What is this?

CYRANO

All there; all but the address.

CHRISTIAN

I—

CYRANO

Oh, you may send it. It will serve.

CHRISTIAN

But why
Have you done this?

CYRANO

I have amused myself
As we all do, we poets—writing vows
To Chloris, Phyllis—any pretty name—
You might have had a pocketful of them!
Take it, and turn to facts my fantasies—
I loosed these loves like doves into the air;
Give them a habitation and a home.
Here, take it— You will find me all the more
Eloquent, being insincere! Come!

CHRISTIAN

First,
There must be a few changes here and there—
Written at random, can it fit Roxane?

CYRANO

Like her own glove.

CHRISTIAN

No, but—

CYRANO

My son, have faith—
Faith in the love of women for themselves—
Roxane will know this letter for her own!

CHRISTIAN

(*Throws himself into the arms of* CYRANO. *They
        stand embraced.*)
My friend!
        (*The door up stage opens a little. A Cadet steals in.*)

THE CADET

Nothing. A silence like the tomb . . .
I hardly dare look—
        (*He sees the two.*)
                        Wha-at?
        (*The Other Cadets crowd in behind him and see.*)

THE CADETS

No!—No!

SECOND CADET

Mon dieu!

THE MUSKETEER

(*Slaps his knee.*)
Well, well, well!

CARBON

Here's our devil . . . Christianized!
Offend one nostril, and he turns the other.

THE MUSKETEER

Now we are allowed to talk about his nose!
   (*Calls*)
Hey, Lise! Come here—
   (*Affectedly*)
                              Snf! What a horrid smell!
What is it? . . .
   (*Plants himself in front of* CYRANO, *and looks at his
   nose in an impolite manner.*)
                       You ought to know about such things;
What seems to have died around here?

CYRANO

(*Knocks him backward over a bench.*)
                                        Cabbage-heads!
(*Joy. The Cadets have found their old* CYRANO
again. General disturbance.)

   (*Curtain*)

THE THIRD ACT

ROXANE'S KISS

A little square in the old Marais: old houses, and a glimpse of narrow streets. On the Right, THE HOUSE OF ROXANE *and her garden wall, overhung with tall shrubbery. Over the door of the house a balcony and a tall window; to one side of the door, a bench.*

Ivy clings to the wall; jasmine embraces the balcony, trembles, and falls away.

By the bench and the jutting stonework of the wall one might easily climb up to the balcony.

Opposite, an ancient house of the like character, brick and stone, whose front door forms an Entrance. The knocker on this door is tied up in linen like an injured thumb.

At the CURTAIN RISE THE DUENNA *is seated on the bench beside the door. The window is wide open on* ROXANE'S *balcony; a light within suggests that it is early evening. By* THE DUENNA *stands* RAGUENEAU *dressed in what might be the livery of one attached to the household. He is by way of telling her something, and wiping his eyes meanwhile.*

RAGUENEAU

—And so she ran off with a Musketeer!
I was ruined— I was alone— Remained
Nothing for me to do but hang myself,
So I did that. Presently along com

147

Monsieur de Bergerac, and cuts me down,
And makes me steward to his cousin.

THE DUENNA

Ruined?—

I thought your pastry was a great success!

RAGUENEAU

(*Shakes his head.*)
Lise loved the soldiers, and I loved the poets—
Mars ate up all the cakes Apollo left;
It did not take long. . . .

THE DUENNA

(*Calls up to window.*)
Roxane! Are you ready?

We are late!

VOICE OF ROXANE

(*Within*)
Putting on my cape—

THE DUENNA

(*To* RAGUENEAU, *indicating the house opposite.*)
Clomire

Across the way receives on Thursday nights—
We are to have a psycho-colloquy
Upon the Tender Passion.

RAGUENEAU

Ah—the Tender . . .

THE DUENNA

(*Sighs*)
—Passion! . . .

(Calls up to window.)
        Roxane!—Hurry, dear—we shall miss
The Tender Passion!

ROXANE
        Coming!—
*(Music of stringed instruments off-stage approach-
ing.)*

THE VOICE OF CYRANO
(Singing)
                La, la, la!—

THE DUENNA
A serenade?—How pleasant—

CYRANO
           No, no, no!—
F natural, you natural born fool!
(Enters, followed by two pages, carrying theorbos.)

FIRST PAGE
(Ironically)
No doubt your honor knows F natural
When he hears—

CYRANO
        I am a musician, infant!—
A pupil of Gassendi.

THE PAGE
(Plays and sings.)
        La, la,—

CYRANO

Here—

Give me that—
> (*He snatches the instrument from the Page and
> continues the tune.*)
>> La, la, la, la—

ROXANE

(*Appears on the Balcony.*)
>>> Is that you

Cyrano?

CYRANO

(*Singing*)
> I, who praise your lilies fair,
But long to love your ro . . . ses!

ROXANE

>>> I'll be down—

Wait—
> (*Goes in through window.*)

THE DUENNA
> Did you train these virtuosi?

CYRANO

>>> No—

I won them on a bet from D'Assoucy.
We were debeating a fine point of grammar
When, pointing out these two young nightingales
Dressed up like peacocks, with their instruments,
He cries: "No, but I KNOW! I'll wager you
A day of music." Well, of course he lost;
And so until to-morrow they are mine,

My private orchestra. Pleasant at first,
But they become a trifle—
   (*To the Pages*)
        Here! Go play
A minuet to Montfleury—and tell him
I sent you!
    (*The Pages go up to the exit.* CYRANO *turns to the*
    Duenna)
     I came here as usual
To inquire after our friend—
    (*To Pages*)
         Play out of tune.
And keep on playing!
    (*The Pages go out. He turns to the Duenna*)
      —Our friend with the great soul.

       ROXANE
   (*Enters in time to hear the last words.*)
He is beautiful and brilliant—and I love him!

       CYRANO
Do you find Christian . . . intellectual?

       ROXANE
More so than you, even.

       CYRANO
    I am glad.

       ROXANE
        No man
Ever so beautifully said those things—
Those pretty nothings that are everything.

Sometimes he falls into a reverie;
His inspiration fails—then all at once,
He will say something absolutely . . . Oh! . . .

CYRANO

Really!

ROXANE

How like a man! You think a man
Who has a handsome face must be a fool.

CYRANO

He talks well about . . . matters of the heart?

ROXANE

He does not *talk;* he rhapsodizes . . . dreams . . .

CYRANO

(*Twisting his moustache.*)
He . . . writes well?

ROXANE

Wonderfully. Listen now:
(*Reciting as from memory.*)
"Take my heart; I shall have it all the more;
Plucking the flowers, we keep the plant in bloom—"
Well?

CYRANO

Pooh!

ROXANE

And this:
"Knowing you have in store
More heart to give than I to find heart-room—"

CYRANO

First he has too much, then too little; just
How much heart does he need?

ROXANE

(*Tapping her foot.*)

You are teasing me!

You are jealous!

CYRANO

(*Startled*)

Jealous?

ROXANE

Of his poetry—

You poets are like that . . .

And these last lines
Are they not the last word in tenderness?—
"There is no more to say: only believe
That unto you my whole heart gives one cry,
And writing, writes down more than you receive;
Sending you kisses through my finger-tips—
Lady, O read my letter with your lips!"

CYRANO

H'm, yes—those last lines . . . but he overwrites!

ROXANE

Listen to this—

CYRANO

You know them all by heart?

ROXANE

Every one!

CYRANO

(*Twisting his moustache.*)
        I may call that flattering . . .

ROXANE

He is a master!

CYRANO

        Oh—come!

ROXANE

                Yes—a master!

CYRANO

        (*Bowing*)
A master—if you will!

THE DUENNA

    (*Comes down stage quickly.*)
                Monsieur de Guiche!—
    (*To* CYRANO, *pushing him toward the house.*)
Go inside—If he does not find you here,
It may be just as well. He may suspect—

ROXANE

—My secret! Yes; he is in love with me
And he is powerful. Let him not know—
One look would frost my roses before bloom.

CYRANO

    (*Going into house.*)
Very well, very well!

ROXANE

    (*To* DE GUICHE, *as he enters*)
                We were just going—

DE GUICHE

I came only to say farewell.

ROXANE

You leave

Paris?

DE GUICHE

Yes—for the front.

ROXANE

Ah!

DE GUICHE

And to-night!

ROXANE

Ah!

DE GUICHE

We have orders to besiege Arras.

ROXANE

Arras?

DE GUICHE

Yes. My departure leaves you . . . cold?

ROXANE

(*Politely*)

Oh! Not that.

DE GUICHE

It has left me desolate—
When shall I see you? Ever? Did you know
I was made Colonel?

ROXANE

(*Indifferent*)

Bravo!

DE GUICHE
Regiment

Of the Guards.

ROXANE
(*Catching her breath.*)
Of the Guards?—

DE GUICHE
His regiment,

Your cousin, the mighty man of words!—
(*Grimly*)

Down there

We may have an accounting!

ROXANE
(*Suffocating*)
Are you sure

The Guards are ordered?

DE GUICHE
Under my command!

ROXANE
(*Sinks down, breathless, on the bench; aside*)
Christian!—

DE GUICHE
What is it?

ROXANE
(*Losing control of herself*)
To the war—perhaps

Never again to— When a woman cares,
Is that nothing?

DE GUICHE

(Surprised and delighted)

You say this now—to me—
Now, at the very moment?—

ROXANE

(Recovers—changes her tone.)

Tell me something:
My cousin— You say you mean to be revenged
On him. Do you mean that?

DE GUICHE

(Smiles)

Why? Would you care?

ROXANE

Not for him.

DE GUICHE

Do you see him?

ROXANE

Now and then,

DE GUICHE

He goes about everywhere nowadays
With one of the Cadets—de Neuve—Neuville—
Neuvillers—

ROXANE

(Coolly)

A tall man?—

DE GUICHE

Blond—

ROXANE

Rosy cheeks?—

DE GUICHE

Handsome!—

ROXANE

Pooh!—

DE GUICHE

And a fool.

ROXANE

(*Languidly*)

So he appears . . .

(*Animated*)

But Cyrano? What will you do to him?
Order him into danger? He loves that!
I know what *I* should do.

DE GUICHE

What?

ROXANE

Leave him here

With his Cadets, while all the regiment
Goes on to glory! That would torture him—
To sit all through the war with folded arms—
I know his nature. If you hate that man,
Strike at his self-esteem.

DE GUICHE

Oh woman—woman!

Who but a woman would have thought of this?

ROXANE

He'll eat his heart out, while his Gascon friends
Bite their nails all day long in Paris here.
And you will be avenged!

DE GUICHE

You love me then,

A little? . . .
    (*She smiles.*)
           Making my enemies your own,
Hating them—I should like to see in that
A sign of love, Roxane.

ROXANE

Perhaps it is one . . .

DE GUICHE

    (*Shows a number of folded despatches.*)
Here are the orders—for each company—
Ready to send . . .
    (*Selects one.*)
          So— This is for the Guards—
I'll keep that. Aha, Cyrano!
    (*To* ROXANE)
             You too,
You play your little games, do you?

ROXANE

    (*Watching him.*)

                Sometimes . . .

DE GUICHE

    (*Close to her, speaking hurriedly.*)
And you!—Oh, I am mad over you!—

Listen—
I leave to-night—but—let you through my hands
Now, when I feel you trembling?—Listen—Close by,
In the Rue d'Orleans, the Capuchins
Have their new convent. By their law, no layman
May pass inside those walls. I'll see to that—
Their sleeves are wide enough to cover me—
The servants of my Uncle-Cardinal
Will fear his nephew. So—I'll come to you
Masked, after everyone knows I have gone—
Oh, let me wait one day!—

ROXANE

If this be known,

Your honor—

DE GUICHE

Bah!

ROXANE

The war—your duty—

DE GUICHE

(*Blows away an imaginary feather.*)

Phoo!—

Only say yes!

ROXANE

No!

DE GUICHE

Whisper . . .

ROXANE

(*Tenderly*)

I ought not

To let you . .

DE GUÏCHE

Ah! . . .

ROXANE

(*Pretends to break down.*)

Ah, go!

(*Aside*)

—Christian remains—

(*Aloud—heroically*)

I must have you a hero—Antoine . . .

DE GUICHE

Heaven! . .

So you can love—

ROXANE

One for whose sake I fear.

DE GUICHE

(*Triumphant*)

I go!

Will that content you?
(*Kisses her hand.*)

ROXANE

Yes—my friend!

(*He goes out.*)

THE DUENNA

(*As* DE GUICHE *disappears, making a deep curtsey behind his back, and imitating* ROXANE's *intense tone.*)

Yes—my friend!

ROXANE

(*Quickly, close to her.*)
    Not a word to Cyrano—
He would never forgive me if he knew
I stole his war!
  (*She calls toward the house.*)
    Cousin!
  (CYRANO *comes out of the house; she turns to him, indicating the house opposite.*)
      We are going over—
Alcandre speaks to-night—and Lysimon.

THE DUENNA

(*Puts finger in her ear.*)
My little finger says we shall not hear
Everything.

CYRANO

  Never mind me—

THE DUENNA

(*Across the street*)
      Look— Oh, look!
The knocker tied up in a napkin— Yes,
They muzzled you because you bark too loud
And interrupt the lecture—little beast!

ROXANE

(*As the door opens*)

Enter . . .

(*To Cyrano*)

If Christian comes, tell him to **wait**.

CYRANO

Oh—

(ROXANE *returns*.)

When he comes, what will you talk about?
You always know beforehand.

ROXANE

About . . .

CYRANO

Well?

ROXANE

You will not tell him, will you?

CYRANO

I am dumb.

ROXANE

About nothing! Or about everything—
I shall say: "Speak of love in your own words—
Improvise! Rhapsodize! Be eloquent!"

CYRANO

(*Smiling*)

Good!

ROXANE

Sh!—

CYRANO

Sh!—

ROXANE

Not a word!
(*She goes in; the door closes.*)

CYRANO

(*Bowing*)

Thank you so much—

ROXANE

(*Opens door and puts out her head.*)
He must be unprepared—

CYRANO

Of course!

ROXANE

Sh!—

(*Goes in again.*)

CYRANO

(*Calls*)

Christian!

(*Christian enters.*)
I have your theme—bring on your memory!—
Here is your chance now to surpass yourself,
No time to lose— Come! Look intelligent—
Come home and learn your lines.

CHRISTIAN

No.

CYRANO

What?

CHRISTIAN

I'll wait

Here for Roxane.

CYRANO

What lunacy is this?
Come quickly!

CHRISTIAN

No, I say! I have had enough—
Taking my words, my letters, all from you—
Making our love a little comedy!
It was a game at first; but now—she cares . . .
Thanks to you. I am not afraid. I'll speak
For myself now.

CYRANO

Undoubtedly!

CHRISTIAN

I will!
Why not? I am no such fool—you shall see!
Besides—my dear friend—you have taught me much;
I ought to know something . . . By God, I know
Enough to take a woman in my arms!
        (ROXANE *appears in the doorway, opposite.*)
There she is now . . . Cyrano, wait! Stay here!

CYRANO

        (*Bows*)
Speak for yourself, my friend!
        (*He goes out.*)

ROXANE

(*Taking leave of the company.*)

—Barthénoide!

Alcandre! . . . Grémione! . . .

THE DUENNA

I told you so—

We missed the Tender Passion!

(*She goes into* ROXANE'S *house.*)

ROXANE

Urimédonte!—

Adieu!

(*As the guests disappear down the street, she turns to* CHRISTIAN.)

Is that you, Christian? Let us stay

Here, in the twilight. They are gone. The air

Is fragrant. We shall be alone. Sit down

There—so . . .

(*They sit on the bench.*)

Now tell me things.

CHRISTIAN

(*After a silence*)

I love you.

ROXANE

(*Closes her eyes.*)

Yes,

Speak to me about love . . .

CHRISTIAN

I love you.

ROXANE

Now

Be eloquent! . . .

CHRISTIAN

I love—

ROXANE

(*Opens her eyes.*)

You have your theme—

Improvise! Rhapsodize!

CHRISTIAN

I love you so!

ROXANE

Of course. And then? . . .

CHRISTIAN

And then . . . Oh, I should be

So happy if you loved me too! Roxane,
Say that you love me too!

ROXANE

(*Making a face.*)

I ask for cream—

You give me milk and water. Tell me first
A little, how you love me.

CHRISTIAN

Very much.

ROXANE

Oh—tell me how you *feel!*

CHRISTIAN

(*Coming nearer, and devouring her with his eyes.*)
                              Your throat . . . If only
I might . . . kiss it—

ROXANE

Christian!

CHRISTIAN

                              I love you so!

ROXANE

(*Makes as if to rise.*)
Again?

CHRISTIAN

(*Desperately, restraining her.*)
              No, not again— I do not love you—

ROXANE

(*Settles back.*)
That is better . . .

CHRISTIAN

I adore you!

ROXANE

                              Oh!—

(*Rises and moves away.*)

CHRISTIAN

                                        I know;
I grow absurd.

ROXANE

(*Coldly*)
              And that displeases me
As much as if you had grown ugly.

CHRISTIAN

I—

ROXANE

Gather your dreams together into words!

CHRISTIAN

I love—

ROXANE

I know; you love me. Adieu.
(*She goes to the house.*)

CHRISTIAN

No,
But wait—please—let me— I was going to say—

ROXANE

(*Pushes the door open.*)
That you adore me. Yes; I know that too.
No! . . . Go away! . . .
(*She goes in and shuts the door in his face.*)

CHRISTIAN

I . . . I . . .

CYRANO

(*Enters*)

A great success!

CHRISTIAN

Help me!

CYRANO

Not I.

CHRISTIAN

I cannot live unless
She loves me—now, this moment!

CYRANO

How the devil
Am I to teach you now—this moment?

CHRISTIAN

(*Catches him by the arm.*)

—Wait!—

Look! Up there!—Quick—
(*The light shows in* ROXANE's *window.*)

CYRANO

Her window—

CHRISTIAN

(*Wailing*)

I shall die!—

CYRANO

Less noise!

CHRISTIAN

Oh, I—

CYRANO

It does seem fairly dark—

CHRISTIAN

(*Excitedly*)
Well?—Well?—Well?—

CYRANO

Let us try what can be done;
It is more than you deserve—stand over there,

Idiot—there!—before the balcony—
Let me stand underneath. I'll whisper you
What to say.

CHRISTIAN

She may hear—she may—

CYRANO

Less noise!

(*The Pages appear up stage.*)

FIRST PAGE

Hep!—

CYRANO

(*Finger to lips*)
Sh!—

FIRST PAGE

(*Low voice*)

We serenaded Montfleury!—
What next?

CYRANO

Down to the corner of the street—
One this way—and the other over there—
If anybody passes, play a tune!

PAGE

What tune, O musical Philosopher?

CYRANO

Sad for a man, or merry for a woman—
Now go!

(*The Pages disappear, one toward each corner of
the street.*)

CYRANO

(*To* CHRISTIAN)
Call her!

CHRISTIAN
Roxane!

CYRANO

Wait . . .
(*Gathers up a handful of pebbles.*)

Gravel . . .
(*Throws it at the window.*)

There!—

ROXANE

(*Opens the window.*)
Who is calling?

CHRISTIAN

I—

ROXANE
Who?

CHRISTIAN
Christian.

ROXANE

You again?

CHRISTIAN

I had to tell you—

CYRANO

(*Under the balcony*)
Good—Keep your voice down. . .

ROXANE

No. Go away. You tell me nothing.

CHRISTIAN

Please!—

ROXANE

You do not love me any more—

CHRISTIAN

(*To whom* CYRANO *whispers his words*)
No—no—
Not any more— I love you . . . evermore . . .
And ever . . . more and more!

ROXANE

(*About to close the window—pauses.*)
A little better . . .

CHRISTIAN

(*Same business*)
Love grows and struggles like . . . an angry child .
Breaking my heart . . . his cradle . . .

ROXANE

(*Coming out on the balcony.*)
Better still—
But . . . such a babe is dangerous; why not
Have smothered it new-born?

CHRISTIAN

(*Same business*)
And so I do . . .
And yet he lives . . . I found . . . as you shall find . . .
This new-born babe . . . an infant . . . Hercules!

ROXANE

(*Further forward*)

Good!—

CHRISTIAN

(*Same business*)

Strong enough . . . at birth . . . to strangle those
Two serpents—Doubt and . . . Pride.

ROXANE

(*Leans over balcony.*)

Why, very well!
Tell me now why you speak so haltingly—
Has your imagination gone lame?

CYRANO

(*Thrusts* CHRISTIAN *under the balcony, and stands
in his place.*)

Here—
This grows too difficult!

ROXANE

Your words to-night
Hesitate. Why?

CYRANO

(*In a low tone, imitating* CHRISTIAN)

Through the warm summer gloom
They grope in darkness toward the light of you.

ROXANE

My words, well aimed, find you more readily.

CYRANO

My heart is open wide and waits for them—
Too large a mark to miss! My words fly home,

Heavy with honey like returning bees,
To your small secret ear. Moreover—yours
Fall to me swiftly. Mine more slowly rise.

ROXANE

Yet not so slowly as they did at first.

CYRANO

They have learned the way, and you have welcomed
them.

ROXANE

(*Softly*)
Am I so far above you now?

CYRANO

So far—
If you let fall upon me one hard word,
Out of that height—you crush me!

ROXANE

(*Turns*)

I'll come down—

CYRANO

(*Quickly*)
No!

ROXANE

(*Points out the bench under the balcony.*)
Stand you on the bench. Come nearer!

CYRANO

(*Recoils into the shadow.*)

No!—

ROXANE

And why—so great a *No?*

CYRANO

(More and more overcome by emotion.)
Let me enjoy
The one moment I ever—my one chance
To speak to you . . . unseen!

ROXANE

Unseen?—

CYRANO

Yes!--yes . . .

Night, making all things dimly beautiful,
One veil over us both— You only see
The darkness of a long cloak in the gloom,
And I the whiteness of a summer gown—
You are all light— I am all shadow! . . . How
Can you know what this moment means to me?
If I was ever eloquent—

ROXANE

You were

Eloquent—

CYRANO

—You have never heard till now
My own heart speaking!

ROXANE

Why not?

CYRANO

Until now,

I spoke through . . .

ROXANE

Yes?—

CYRANO

—through that sweet drunkenness
You pour into the world out of your eyes!
But to-night . . . But to-night, I indeed speak
For the first time!

ROXANE

For the first time— Your voice,
Even, is not the same.

CYRANO

(*Passionately; moves nearer.*)
How should it be?
I have another voice to-night—my own,
Myself, daring—
(*He stops, confused; then tries to recover himself.*)
Where was I? . . . I forget! . . .
Forgive me. This is all sweet like a dream . . .
Strange—like a dream . . .

ROXANE

How, strange?

CYRANO

Is it not so
To be myself to you, and have no fear
Of moving you to laughter?

ROXANE
Laughter— why?

CYRANO
(*Struggling for an explanation.*)
Because . . . What am I . . . What is any man,
That he dare ask for you? Therefore my heart
Hides behind phrases. There's a modesty
In these things too— I come here to pluck down
Out of the sky the evening star—then smile,
And stoop to gather little flowers.

ROXANE
Are they
Not sweet, those little flowers?

CYRANO
Not enough sweet
For you and me, to-night!

ROXANE
(*Breathless*)
You never spoke
To me like this . . .

CYRANO
Little things, pretty things—
Arrows and hearts and torches—roses red,
And violets blue—are these all? Come away,
And breathe fresh air! Must we keep on and on
Sipping stale honey out of tiny cups
Decorated with golden tracery,
Drop by drop, all day long? We are alive;

We thirst— Come away, plunge, and drink, and drown
In the great river flowing to the sea!

ROXANE

But . . . Poetry?

CYRANO

I have made rimes for you—
Not now— Shall we insult Nature, this night,
These flowers, this moment—shall we set all these
To phrases from a letter by Voiture?
Look once at the high stars that shine in heaven,
And put off artificiality!
Have you not seen great gaudy hothouse flowers,
Barren, without fragrance?—Souls are like that:
Forced to show all, they soon become all show—
The means to Nature's end ends meaningless!

ROXANE

But . . . Poetry?

CYRANO

Love hates that game of words!
It is a crime to fence with life— I tell you,
There comes one moment, once—and God help those
Who pass that moment by!—when Beauty stands
Looking into the soul with grave, sweet eyes
That sicken at pretty words!

ROXANE

If that be true—
And when that moment comes to you and me—
What words will you? . . .

CYRANO

All those, all those, all those
That blossom in my heart, I'll fling to you—
Armfuls of loose bloom! Love, I love beyond
Breath, beyond reason, beyond love's own power
Of loving! Your name is like a golden bell
Hung in my heart; and when I think of you,
I tremble, and the bell swings and rings—

Roxane! . . .

Roxane! .   along my veins, *Roxane!*   .

I know
All small forgotten things that once meant You—
I remember last year, the First of May,
A little before noon, you had your hair
Drawn low, that one time only. Is that strange?
You know how, after looking at the sun,
One sees red suns everywhere—so, for hours
After the flood of sunshine that you are,
My eyes are blinded by your burning hair!

ROXANE

(*Very low*)
Yes . . . that is . . . Love—

CYRANO

Yes, that is Love—that wind
Of terrible and jealous beauty, blowing
Over me—that dark fire, that music . . .

Yet
Love seeketh not his own! Dear, you may take
My happiness to make you happier,

Even though you never know I gave it you—
Only let me hear sometimes, all alone,
The distant laughter of your joy! . . .

I never

Look at you, but there's some new virtue born
In me, some new courage. Do you begin
To understand, a little? Can you feel
My soul, there in the darkness, breathe on you?
—Oh, but to-night, now, I dare say these things—
I . . . to you . . . and you hear them! . . . It is **too**
    much!
In my most sweet unreasonable dreams,
I have not hoped for this! Now let me die,
Having lived. It is my voice, mine, my own,
That makes you tremble there in the green gloom
Above me—for you do tremble, as a blossom
Among the leaves— You tremble, and I can feel,
All the way down along these jasmine branches,
Whether you will or no, the passion of you
Trembling . . .

> (*He kisses wildly the end of a drooping spray of
> jasmine.*)

ROXANE

Yes, I do tremble . . . and I weep . . .

And I love you . . . and I am yours . . . and you
Have made me thus!

CYRANO

(*After a pause; quietly.*)

What is death like, I wonder?

I know everything else now . . .

                            I have done

This, to you—I, myself . . .

                        Only let me

Ask one thing more—

CHRISTIAN

(Under the balcony)
                        One kiss!

ROXANE

(Startled)

                                One?—

CYRANO

(To CHRISTIAN)

                                You! . . .

ROXANE

                                You ask me

For—

CYRANO

    I . . . Yes, but—I mean—
    (To CHRISTIAN)

                        You go too far!

CHRISTIAN

She is willing!—Why not make the most of it?

CYRANO

    (To ROXANE)
I did ask . . . but I know I ask too much . . .

ROXANE

Only one— Is that all?

CYRANO

All!—How much more
Than all!—I know—I frighten you—I ask . . .
I ask you to refuse—

CHRISTIAN

(*To* CYRANO)
But why? Why? Why?

CYRANO

Christian, be quiet!

ROXANE

(*Leaning over*)
What is that you say
To yourself?

CYRANO

I am angry with myself
Because I go too far, and so I say
To myself: "Christian, be quiet!"
(*The theorbos begin to play.*)
Hark—someone
Is coming—
(ROXANE *closes her window.* CYRANO *listens to the
theorbos, one of which plays a gay melody, the
other a mournful one.*)
A sad tune, a merry tune—
Man, woman—what do they mean?—
(*A Capuchin enters; he carries a lantern, and goes
from house to house, looking at the doors.*)
Aha!—a priest!

(*To the Capuchin*)
What is this new game of Diogenes?

THE CAPUCHIN
I am looking for the house of Madame—

CHRISTIAN
(*Impatient*)

Bah!—

THE CAPUCHIN
Madeleine Robin—

CHRISTIAN
What does he want?

CYRANO
(*To the Capuchin; points out a street.*)

This way—
To the right—keep to the right—

THE CAPUCHIN
I thank you, sir!—
I'll say my beads for you to the last grain.

CYRANO
Good fortune, father, and my service to you!
(*The Capuchin goes out*)

CHRISTIAN
Win me that kiss!

CYRANO
No.

CHRISTIAN
Sooner or later—

CYRANO

True . . .

That is true . . . Soon or late, it will be so
Because you are young and she is beautiful—
 (*To himself*)
Since it must be, I had rather be myself
 (*The window re-opens.* CHRISTIAN *hides under
 the balcony.*)
The cause of . . . what must be.

ROXANE

 (*Out on the balcony*)

Are you still there?

We were speaking of—

CYRANO

A kiss. The word is sweet—
What will the deed be? Are your lips afraid
Even of its burning name? Not much afraid—
Not too much! Have you not unwittingly
Laid aside laughter, slipping beyond speech
Insensibly, already, without fear,
From words to smiles . . . from smiles to sighs . . .
 from sighing,
Even to tears? One step more—only one—
From a tear to a kiss—one step, one thrill!

ROXANE

Hush!—

CYRANO

And what is a kiss, when all is done?
A promise given under seal— a vow

Taken before the shrine of memory—
A signature acknowledged—a rosy dot
Over the i of Loving—a secret whispered
To listening lips apart—a moment made
Immortal, with a rush of wings unseen—
A sacrament of blossoms, a new song
Sung by two hearts to an old simple tune—
The ring of one horizon around two souls
Together, all alone!

ROXANE
Hush! . . .

CYRANO
Why, what shame?—
There was a Queen of France, not long ago,
And a great lord of England—a queen's gift,
A crown jewel!—

ROXANE
Indeed!

CYRANO
Indeed, like him,
I have my sorrows and my silences;
Like her, you are the queen I dare adore;
Like him I am faithful and forlorn—

ROXANE
Like him,
Beautiful—

CYRANO
(*Aside*)
So I am—I forgot that!

ROXANE

Then—Come! . . . Gather your sacred blossom . . .

CYRANO

(*To* CHRISTIAN)

Go!—

ROXANE

Your crown jewel . . .

CYRANO

Go on!—

ROXANE

Your old new song . . .

CYRANO

Climb!—

CHRISTIAN

(*Hesitates*)

No— Would you?—not yet—

ROXANE

Your moment made

Immortal . . .

CYRANO

(*Pushing him.*)

Climb up, animal!

(CHRISTIAN *springs on the bench, and climbs by the pillars, the branches, the vines, until he bestrides the balcony railing.*)

CHRISTIAN

Roxane! . . .

(*He takes her in his arms and bends over her.*

CYRANO

>   (*Very low*)
> Ah! . . . Roxane! . . .
>
>   I have won what I have won—
> The feast of love—and I am Lazarus!
> Yet . . . I have something here that is mine now
> And was not mine before I spoke the words
> That won her—not for me! . . . Kissing my words
> My words, upon your lips!
>   (*The theorbos begin to play.*)
>   A merry tune—
> A sad tune— So! The Capuchin!
>   (*He pretends to be running, as if he had arrived
>   from a distance; then calls up to the balcony.*)
>   Holo!

ROXANE

Who is it?

CYRANO

>   I. Is Christian there with you?

CHRISTIAN

>   (*Astonished*)
> Cyrano!

ROXANE

>   Good morrow, Cousin!

CYRANO

>   Cousin, . . . good morrow!

ROXANE

I am coming down.
>   (*She disappears into the house. The Capuchin en-
>   ters up stage.*)

CHRISTIAN

(*Sees him.*)

Oh—again!

THE CAPUCHIN

(*To* CYRANO)

She lives *here,*

Madeleine Robin!

CYRANO

You said RO-LIN.

THE CAPUCHIN

No—

R-O-B-I-N

ROXANE

(*Appears on the threshold of the house, followed by* RAGUENEAU *with a lantern, and by* CHRISTIAN.)

What is it?

THE CAPUCHIN

A letter.

CHRISTIAN

Oh! . . .

THE CAPUCHIN

(*To* ROXANE)

Some matter profitable to the soul—
A very noble lord gave it to me!

ROXANE

(*To* CHRISTIAN)

De Guiche!

CHRISTIAN

He dares?—

ROXANE

It will not be for long;
When he learns that I love you . . .

(*By the light of the lantern which* RAGUENEAU
*holds, she reads the letter in a low tone, as if to
herself.*)

"Mademoiselle
The drums are beating, and the regiment
Arms for the march. Secretly I remain
Here, in the Convent. I have disobeyed;
I shall be with you soon. I send this first
By an old monk, as simple as a sheep,
Who understands nothing of this. Your smile
Is more than I can bear, and seek no more.
Be alone to-night, waiting for one who dares
To hope you will forgive . . . —" etcetera—

(*To the Capuchin*)

Father, this letter concerns you . . .

(*To* CHRISTIAN)

—and you.

Listen:

(*The others gather around her. She pretends to
read from the letter, aloud.*)

"Mademoiselle:
The Cardinal
Will have his way, although against your will;
That is why I am sending this to you
By a most holy man, intelligent,

Discreet. You will communicate to him
Our order to perform, here and at once
The rite of . . .
     (*Turns the page*)
          —Holy Matrimony. You
And Christian will be married privately
In your house. I have sent him to you. I know
You hesitate. Be resigned, nevertheless,
To the Cardinal's command, who sends herewith
His blessing. Be assured also of my own
Respect and high consideration—*signed,*
Your very humble and—etcetera—"

THE CAPUCHIN

A noble lord! I said so—never fear—
A worthy lord!—a very worthy lord!—

ROXANE

    (*To* CHRISTIAN)
Am I a good reader of letters?

CHRISTIAN

    (*Motions toward the Capuchin.*)
              Careful!—

ROXANE

    (*In a tragic tone*)
Oh, this is terrible!

THE CAPUCHIN

    (*Turns the light of his lantern on* CYRANO.)
          You are to be—

CHRISTIAN

I am the bridegroom!

THE CAPUCHIN

(*Turns his lantern upon* CHRISTIAN; *then, as if some suspicion crossed his mind, upon seeing the young man so handsome.*)
Oh—why, *you* . . .

ROXANE

(*Quickly*)

Look here—

"*Postscript:* Give to the Convent in my name
One hundred and twenty pistoles"—

THE CAPUCHIN

Think of it!

A worthy lord—a very worthy lord! . . .
(*To* ROXANE, *solemnly*)
Daughter, resign yourself!

ROXANE

(*With an air of martyrdom*)
I am resigned . . .
(*While* RAGUENEAU *opens the door for the Capuchin and* CHRISTIAN *invites him to enter, she turns to* CYRANO.)
De Guiche may come. Keep him out here with you.
Do not let him—

CYRANO

I understand!
(*To the Capuchin*)

How long

Will you be?—

THE CAPUCHIN
Oh, a quarter of an hour.

CYRANO
(Hurrying them into the house.)
Hurry—I'll wait here—

ROXANE
(To CHRISTIAN)
Come!
(They go into the house.)

CYRANO
Now then, to make
His Grace delay that quarter of an hour . . .
I have it!—up here—
*(He steps on the bench, and climbs up the wall
toward the balcony. The theorbos begin to play
a mournful melody.)*
Sad music— Ah, a man! . . .
(The music pauses on a sinister tremolo.)
Oh—very much a man!
*(He sits astride of the railing, and, drawing toward
him a long branch of one of the trees which bor-
der the garden wall, he grasps it with both
hands, ready to swing himself down.)*
So—not too high—
(He peers down at the ground.)
I must float gently through the atmosphere—

DE GUICHE

(Enters, masked, groping in the dark toward the house.)

Where is that cursed, bleating Capuchin?

CYRANO

What if he knows my voice?—the devil!—Tic-tac,
Bergerac—we unlock our Gascon tongue;
A good strong accent--

DE GUICHE

Here is the house—all dark—
Damn this mask!—

(As he is about to enter the house, CYRANO leaps from the balcony, still holding fast to the branch, which bends and swings him between DE GUICHE and the door; then he releases the branch and pretends to fall heavily as though from a height. He lands flatlong on the ground, where he lies motionless, as if stunned. DE GUICHE leaps back.)

What is that?

(When he lifts his eyes, the branch has sprung back into place. He can see nothing but the sky; he does not understand.)

Why . . . where did this man
Fall from?

CYRANO

(Sits up, and speaks with a strong accent.)
—The moon!

DE GUICHE

You—

CYRANO

From the moon, the moon!
I fell out of the moon!

DE GUICHE

The fellow is mad—

CYRANO

(*Dreamily*)
Where am I?

DE GUICHE

Why—

CYRANO

What time is it? What place
Is this? What day? What season?

DE GUICHE

You—

CYRANO

I am stunned!

DE GUICHE

My dear sir—

CYRANO

Like a bomb—a bomb—I fell
From the moon!

DE GUICHE

Now, see here—

CYRANO

(*Rising to his feet, and speaking in a terrible voice.*)

I say, the moon!

DE GUICHE

(*Recoils*)

Very well—if you say so—
(*Aside*)

Raving mad!—

CYRANO

(*Advancing upon him.*)
I am not speaking metaphorically!

DE GUICHE

Pardon.

CYRANO

A hundred years—an hour ago—
I really cannot say how long I fell—
I was in yonder shining sphere—

DE GUICHE

(*Shrugs*)

Quite so.

Please let me pass.

CYRANO

(*Interposes himself.*)

Where am I? Tell the truth—
I can bear it. In what quarter of the globe
Have I descended like a meteorite?

DE GUICHE

Morbleu!

CYRANO

⏉ could not choose my place to fall—
The earth spun round so fast— Was it the Earth,
I wonder?—Or is this another world?
Another moon? Whither have I been drawn
By the dead weight of my posterior?

DE GUICHE

Sir, I repeat—

CYRANO

(*With a sudden cry, which causes* DE GUICHE *to
recoil again.*)
His face! My God—black!

DE GUICHE

(*Carries his hand to his mask.*)

Oh—

CYRANO

(*Terrified*)
Are you a native? Is this Africa?

DE GUICHE

—This mask!

CYRANO

(*Somewhat reassured*)
Are we in Venice? Genoa?

DE GUICHE

(*Tries to pass him.*)
A lady is waiting for me.

CYRANO

(*Quite happy again.*)
So this is Paris!

DE GUICHE

(*Smiling in spite of himself.*)
This fool becomes amusing.

CYRANO

Ah! You smile?

DE GUICHE

I do. Kindly permit me—

CYRANO

(*Delighted*)

Dear old Paris—

Well, well!—
　　　(*Wholly at his ease, smiles, bows, arranges his
　　　dress.*)
　　　　　　Excuse my appearance. I arrive
By the last thunderbolt—a trifle singed
As I came through the ether. These long journeys—
You know! There are so few conveniences!
My eyes are full of star-dust. On my spurs,
Some sort of fur . . . Planet's apparently . . .
　　　(*Plucks something from his sleeve.*)
Look—on my doublet— That's a Comet's hair!
　　　(*He blows something from the back of his hand.*)
Phoo!

DE GUICHE

(*Grows angry.*)
　　Monsieur—

CYRANO

(*As* DE GUICHE *is about to push past, thrusts his
　　leg in the way.*)

Here's a tooth, stuck in my boot,
From the Great Bear. Trying to get away,
I tripped over the Scorpion and came down
Slap, into one scale of the Balances—
The pointer marks my weight this moment . . .
    (*Pointing upward.*)

See?

    (De Guiche *makes a sudden movement.* Cyrano
        catches his arm.)
Be careful! If you struck me on the nose,
It would drip milk!

DE GUICHE
Milk?

CYRANO
From the Milky Way!

DE GUICHE
Hell!

CYRANO
No, no—Heaven.
    (*Crossing his arms*)
                Curious place up there—
Did you know Sirius wore a nightcap? True!
    (*Confidentially*)
The Little Bear is still too young to bite.
    (*Laughing*)
My foot caught in the Lyre, and broke a string.
    (*Proudly*)
Well—when I write my book, and tell the tale
Of my adventures—all these little stars

That shake out of my cloak—I must save those
To use for asterisks!

DE GUICHE

That will do now—

I wish—

CYRANO

Yes, yes—I know—

DE GUICHE

Sir—

CYRANO

You desire

To learn from my own lips the character
Of the moon's surface—its inhabitants
If any—

DE GUICHE

(*Loses patience and shouts.*)
I desire no such thing! I—

CYRANO

(*Rapidly*)
You wish to know by what mysterious means
I reached the moon?—well—confidentially—
It was a new invention of my own.

DE GUICHE

(*Discouraged*)
Drunk too—as well as mad!

CYRANO

I scorned the eagle

Of Regiomontanus, and the dove
Of Archytas!

DE GUICHE
A learned lunatic!—

CYRANO
I imitated no one. I myself
Discovered not one scheme merely, but six—
Six ways to violate the virgin sky!

(DE GUICHE *has succeeded in passing him, and
moves toward the door of* ROXANE'S *house.* CY-
RANO *follows, ready to use violence if necessary.*)

DE GUICHE
(*Looks around.*)
Six?

CYRANO
(*With increasing volubility*)
As for instance—Having stripped **myself**
Bare as a wax candle, adorn my form
With crystal vials filled with morning **dew**,
And so be drawn aloft, as the sun rises
Drinking the mist of dawn!

DE GUICHE
(*Takes a step toward* CYRANO.)
Yes—that makes **one**.

CYRANO
(*Draws back to lead him away from the door;
speaks faster and faster.*)
Or, sealing up the air in a cedar chest,

Rarefy it by means of mirrors, placed
In an icosahedron.

DE GUICHE
        (*Takes another step.*)
                Two.

CYRANO
        (*Still retreating*)
                        Again,
I might construct a rocket, in the form
Of a huge locust, driven by impulses
Of villainous saltpetre from the rear,
Upward, by leaps and bounds.

DE GUICHE
        (*Interested in spite of himself, and counting on his
            fingers.*)
                        Three.

CYRANO
        (*Same business*)
                        Or again,
Smoke having a natural tendency to rise,
Blow in a globe enough to raise me.

DE GUICHE
        (*Same business, more and more astonished.*)
                        Four!

CYRANO
Or since Diana, as old fables tell,
Draws forth to fill her crescent horn, the marrow
Of bulls and goats—to anoint myself therewith.

DE GUICHE

(Hypnotized)

Five!—

CYRANO

*(Has by this time led him all the way across the
    street, close to a bench.)*
                Finally—seated on an iron plate,
To hurl a magnet in the air—the iron
Follows—I catch the magnet—throw again—
And so proceed indefinitely.

DE GUICHE

                Six!—

All excellent,—and which did you adopt?

CYRANO

(Coolly)

Why, none of them. . . . A seventh.

DE GUICHE

                                Which was?—

CYRANO

                                        Guess!—

DE GUICHE

An interesting idiot, this!

CYRANO

*(Imitates the sound of waves with his voice, and
    their movement by large, vague gestures.)*
                Hoo! . . . Hoo! . . .

DE GUICHE

Well?

CYRANO

Have you guessed it yet?

DE GUICHE

Why, no.

CYRANO

(*Grandiloquent*)

The ocean! . . .

What hour its rising tide seeks the full moon,
I laid me on the strand, fresh from the spray,
My head fronting the moonbeams, since the hair
Retains moisture—and so I slowly rose
As upon angels' wings, effortlessly,
Upward—then suddenly I felt a shock!—
And then . . .

DE GUICHE

(*Overcome by curiosity, sits down on the bench.*)
And then?

CYRANO

And then—
(*Changes abruptly to his natural voice.*)
The time is up!—
Fifteen minutes, your Grace!—You are now free;
And—they are bound—in wedlock.

DE GUICHE

(*Leaping up*)

Am *I* drunk?
That voice . . .
(*The door of* ROXANE's *house opens; lackeys ap-*

pear, bearing lighted candles. Lights Up. Cyrano
removes his hat.)

And that nose!—Cyrano!

CYRANO

(*Saluting*)

Cyrano! . . .

This very moment, they have exchanged rings.

DE GUICHE

Who?

(*He turns up stage.* Tableau: *between the lackeys,*
Roxane *and* Christian *appear, hand in hand.
The Capuchin follows them, smiling.* Ragueneau
*holds aloft a torch. The Duenna brings up the
rear, in a negligée, and a pleasant flutter of emotion.*)

Zounds!

(*To* Roxane)

You?—

(*Recognizes* Christian)

He?—

(*Saluting* Roxane)

My sincere compliments!

(*To* Cyrano)

You also, my inventor of machines!
Your rigmarole would have detained a saint
Entering Paradise—decidedly
You must not fail to write that book some day!

CYRANO

(*Bowing*)

Sir, I engage myself to do so.

(Leads the bridal pair down to DE GUICHE *and strokes with great satisfaction his long white beard.)*

My lord,
The handsome couple you—and God—have joined
Together!

DE GUICHE

(Regarding him with a frosty eye.)
Quite so.
(Turns to ROXANE)
Madame, kindly bid
Your . . . husband farewell.

ROXANE
Oh!—

DE GUICHE

(To CHRISTIAN)

Your regiment
Leaves to-night, sir. Report at once!

ROXANE

You mean
For the front? The war?

DE GUICHE
Certainly!

ROXANE

I thought
The Cadets were not going—

DE GUICHE
Oh yes, they are!

(Taking out the despatch from his pocket.)
Here is the order—
    (To CHRISTIAN*)*
                Baron! Deliver this.

ROXANE
(Throws herself into CHRISTIAN's *arms.)*
Christian!

DE GUICHE
    (To CYRANO, *sneering)*
        The bridal night is not so near!

CYRANO
    (Aside)
Somehow that news fails to disquiet me.

CHRISTIAN
    (To ROXANE*)*
Your lips again . . .

CYRANO
          There . . . That will do now— Come!

CHRISTIAN
    (Still holding ROXANE*)*
You do not know how hard it is—

CYRANO
    (Tries to drag him away.)
                I know!
    (The beating of drums is heard in the distance.)

DE GUICHE
    (Up stage)
The regiment—on the march!

ROXANE

(*As* Cyrano *tries to lead* Christian *away, follows,
    and detains them.*)
                                            Take care of him
For me—
    (*Appealingly*)
            Promise me never to let him do
Anything dangerous!

CYRANO

I'll do my best—

I cannot promise—

ROXANE

(*Same business*)
            Make him be careful!

CYRANO

                                            Yes—

I'll try—

ROXANE

(*Same business*)
            Be sure you keep him dry and warm!

CYRANO

Yes, yes—if possible—

ROXANE

(*Same business; confidentially, in his ear*)
            See that he remains
Faithful—

CYRANO

Of course! If—

ROXANE

(Same business)

And have him write to me
Every single day.

CYRANO

(Stops)

That, I promise you!

(Curtain)

THE FOURTH ACT

THE CADETS OF GASCOYNE

THE POST *occupied by the Company of* CARBON DE CASTEL-JALOUX *at* THE SIEGE OF ARRAS.

In the background, a Rampart traversing the entire scene; beyond this, and apparently below, a Plain stretches away to the horizon. The country is cut up with earth-works and other suggestions of the siege. In the distance against the sky-line, the houses and the walls of Arras.

Tents; scattered Weapons; Drums, etcetera. It is near day-break, and the East is yellow with approaching dawn. Sentries at intervals. Camp-fires.

CURTAIN RISE *discovers the Cadets asleep, rolled in their cloaks.* CARBON DE CASTEL-JALOUX *and* LE BRET *keep watch. They are both very thin and pale.* CHRISTIAN *is asleep among the others, wrapped in his cloak, in the fore-ground, his face lighted by the flickering fire. Silence.*

LE BRET

Horrible!

CARBON

Why, yes. All of that.

LE BRET

Mordious!

CARBON

(Gesture toward the sleeping Cadets)
Swear gently— You might wake them.
(To Cadets)

213

Go to sleep—

Hush!
> (*To* LE BRET)
> Who sleeps dines.

CARBON
LE BRET
                    I have insomnia.

God! What a famine.
> (*Firing off stage.*)

CARBON
                    Curse that musketry!

They'll wake my babies.
> (*To the men*)

Go to sleep!—

A CADET
> (*Rouses*)
                                        Diantre!

Again?

CARBON
No—only Cyrano coming home.
> (*The heads which have been raised sink back
> again.*)

A SENTRY
> (*Off stage*)

Halt! Who goes there?

VOICE OF CYRANO
                    Bergerac!

THE SENTRY ON THE PARAPET
                    Halt! Who goes?—

CYRANO

(*Appears on the parapet.*)

Bergerac, idiot!

LE BRET

(*Goes to meet him.*)
                    Thank God again!

CYRANO

(*Signs to him not to wake anyone.*)

Hush!

LE BRET

        Wounded?—

CYRANO

                    No— They always miss me—quite

A habit by this time!

LE BRET

                    Yes— Go right on—

Risk your life every morning before breakfast

To send a letter!

CYRANO

(*Stops near* CHRISTIAN.)
                    I promised he should write

Every single day . . .

        (*Looks down at him.*)

                    Hm— The boy looks pale

When he is asleep—thin too—starving to death—

If that poor child knew! Handsome, none the less . . .

LE BRET

Go and get some sleep!

CYRANO

(*Affectionately*)

Now, now—you old **bear,**
No growling!—I am careful—you know I am—
Every night, when I cross the Spanish lines
I wait till they are all drunk.

LE BRET

You might bring
Something with you.

CYRANO

I have to travel light
To pass through— By the way, there will **be news**
For you to-day; the French will eat or die,
If what I saw means anything.

LE BRET

Tell us!

CYRANO

No—
I am not sure—we shall see!

CARBON

What a war,
When the besiegers starve to death!

LE BRET

Fine **war—**
Fine situation! We besiege Arras—
The Cardinal Prince of Spain besieges us—
And—here we are!

CYRANO

Someone might besiege *him*.

CARBON

A hungry joke!

CYRANO

Ho, ho!

LE BRET

Yes, you can laugh—
Risking a life like yours to carry letters—
Where are you going now?

CYRANO

(*At the tent door*)

To write another.

(*Goes into tent.*)

(*A little more daylight. The clouds redden. The
town of Arras shows on the horizon. A cannon
shot is heard, followed immediately by a roll of
drums, far away to the left. Other drums beat a
little nearer. The drums go on answering each
other here and there, approach, beat loudly almost on the stage, and die away toward the right,
across the camp. The camp awakes. Voices of
officers in the distance.*)

CARBON

(*Sighs*)

Those drums!—another good nourishing sleep
Gone to the devil.

(*The Cadets rouse themselves.*)

Now then!—

FIRST CADET

(*Sits up, yawns.*)

God! I'm hungry!

SECOND CADET

Starving!

ALL

(*Groan*)
Aoh!

CARBON

Up with you!

THIRD CADET

Not another step!

FOURTH CADET

Not another movement!

FIRST CADET

Look at my tongue—
I said this air was indigestible!

FIFTH CADET

My coronet for half a pound of cheese!

SIXTH CADET

I have no stomach for this war— I'll stay
In my tent—like Achilles.

ANOTHER

Yes—no bread,
No fighting—

CARBON

Cyrano!

OTHERS

May as well die—

CARBON

Come out here!—You know how to talk to them.
Get them laughing—

SECOND CADET

(*Rushes up to First Cadet who is eating some-*
thing.)

What are you gnawing there?

FIRST CADET

Gun wads and axle-grease. Fat country this
Around Arras.

ANOTHER

(*Enters*)

I have been out hunting!

ANOTHER

(*Enters*)

I

Went fishing, in the Scarpe!

ALL

(*Leaping up and surrounding the newcomers.*)

Find anything?
Any fish? Any game? Perch? Partridges?
Let me look!

THE FISHERMAN

Yes—one gudgeon.

(*Shows it.*)

THE HUNTER

One fat . . . sparrow.

(Shows it.)

ALL

Ah!—See here, this—mutiny!—

CARBON

Cyrano!

Come and help!

CYRANO

(Enters from tent.)
Well?
(Silence. To the First Cadet who is walking away, with his chin on his chest.)
You there, with the long face?

FIRST CADET

I have something on my mind that troubles me.

CYRANO

What is that?

FIRST CADET

My stomach.

CYRANO

So have I.

FIRST CADET

No doubt

You enjoy this!

CYRANO

(Tightens his belt.)
It keeps me looking young.

SECOND CADET

My teeth are growing rusty.

CYRANO

Sharpen them!

THIRD CADET

My belly sounds as hollow as a drum.

CYRANO

Beat the long roll on it!

FOURTH CADET

My ears are ringing.

CYRANO

Liar! A hungry belly has no ears.

FIFTH CADET

Oh for a barrel of good wine!

CYRANO

(Offers him his own helmet.)

Your casque.

SIXTH CADET

I'll swallow anything!

CYRANO

(Throws him the book which he has in his hand.)

Try the *Iliad*.

SEVENTH CADET

The Cardinal, he has four meals a day—
What does he care!

CYRANO

Ask him; he really ought
To send you . . . a spring lamb out of his flock,
Roasted whole—

THE CADET

Yes, and a bottle—

CYRANO

(*Exaggerates the manner of one speaking to a servant.*)

If you please,
Richelieu—a little more of the Red Seal . . .
Ah, thank you!

THE CADET

And the salad—

CYRANO

Of course—Romaine!

ANOTHER CADET

(*Shivering*)
I am as hungry as a wolf.

CYRANO

(*Tosses him a cloak.*)
Put on
Your sheep's clothing.

FIRST CADET

(*With a shrug*)
Always the clever answer!

CYRANO

Always the answer—yes! Let me die so—
Under some rosy-golden sunset, saying

A good thing, for a good cause! By the sword,
The point of honor—by the hand of one
Worthy to be my foeman, let me fall—
Steel in my heart, and laughter on my lips!

VOICES HERE AND THERE

All very well— We are hungry!

CYRANO

Bah! You think
Of nothing but yourselves.

(*His eye singles out the old fifer in the background.*)

Here, Bertrandou,
You were a shepherd once— Your pipe now! Come,
Breathe, blow,— Play to these belly-worshippers
The old airs of the South—

*Airs with a smile in them,
Airs with a sigh in them, airs with the breeze
And the blue of the sky in them—*

Small, demure tunes
Whose every note is like a little sister—
Songs heard only in some long silent voice
Not quite forgotten— Mountain melodies
Like thin smoke rising from brown cottages
In the still noon, slowly— Quaint lullabies,
Whose very music has a Southern tongue—

(*The old man sits down and prepares his fife.*)

Now let the fife, that dry old warrior,
Dream, while over the stops your fingers dance
A minuet of little birds—let him

Dream beyond ebony and ivory;
Let him remember he was once a reed
Out of the river, and recall the spirit
Of innocent, untroubled country days . . .
        (*The fifer begins to play a Provençal melody.*)
Listen, you Gascons! Now it is no more
The shrill fife— It is the flute, through woodlands far
Away, calling—no longer the hot battle-cry,
But the cool, quiet pipe our goatherds play!
Listen—the forest glens . . . the hills . . . the downs . . .
The green sweetness of night on the Dordogne . . .
Listen, you Gascons! It is all Gascoyne! . . .
        (*Every head is bowed; every eye cast down. Here
        and there a tear is furtively brushed away with
        the back of a hand, the corner of a cloak.*)

CARBON

(*Softly to* CYRANO)
You make them weep—

CYRANO

                        For homesickness—a hunger
More noble than that hunger of the flesh;
It is their hearts now that are starving.

CARBON

                                    Yes,
But you melt down their manhood.

CYRANO

(*Motions the drummer to approach.*)
                                    You think so?
Let them be. There is iron in their blood

Not easily dissolved in tears. You need
Only—

    (*He makes a gesture; the drum beats.*)

ALL

    (*Spring up and rush toward their weapons.*)
      What's that? Where is it?—What?—

CYRANO

    (*Smiles*)

                        You see—
Let Mars snore in his sleep once—and farewell
Venus—sweet dreams—regrets—dear thoughts of home—
All the fife lulls to rest wakes at the drums!

A CADET

    (*Looks up stage.*)
Aha— Monsieur de Guiche!

THE CADETS

    (*Mutter among themselves.*)
               Ugh! . . .

CYRANO

    (*Smiles*)

                        Flattering
Murmur!

A CADET

    He makes me weary!

ANOTHER

               With his collar
Of lace over his corselet—

ANOTHER
                    Like a ribbon
Tied round a sword!

ANOTHER
                    Bandages for a boil
On the back of his neck—

SECOND CADET
                    A courtier always!

ANOTHER
The Cardinal's nephew!

CARBON
                    None the less—a Gascon.

FIRST CADET
A counterfeit! Never you trust that man—
Because we Gascons, look you, are all mad—
This fellow is reasonable—nothing more
Dangerous than a reasonable Gascon!

LE BRET
He looks pale.

ANOTHER
                    Oh, he can be hungry too,
Like any other poor devil—but he wears
So many jewels on that belt of his
That his cramps glitter in the sun!

CYRANO

    (Quickly)

                              Is he

To see us looking miserable? Quick—
Pipes!—Cards!—Dice!—

> (*They all hurriedly begin to play, on their stools,
> on the drums, or on their cloaks spread on the
> ground, lighting their long pipes meanwhile.*)

As for me, I read Descartes.

> (*He walks up and down, reading a small book
> which he takes from his pocket.* TABLEAU: DE
> GUICHE *enters, looking pale and haggard. All
> are absorbed in their games. General air of con-
> tentment.* DE GUICHE *goes to* CARBON. *They look
> at each other askance, each observing with satis-
> faction the condition of the other.*)

DE GUICHE

Good morning!
> (*Aside*)

He looks yellow.

CARBON

> (*Same business*)

He is all eyes.

DE GUICHE

> (*Looks at the Cadets.*)

What have we here? Black looks? Yes, gentlemen—
I am informed I am not popular;
The hill-nobility, barons of Béarn,
The pomp and pride of Périgord—I learn
They disapprove their colonel; call him courtier,
Politician—they take it ill that I
Cover my steel with lace of Genoa.

It is a great offense to be a Gascon
And not to be a beggar!
    (*Silence. They smoke. They play.*)
                      Well— Shall I have
Your captain punish you? . . . No.

CARBON

                          As to that,
It would be impossible.

DE GUICHE

      Oh?

CARBON

                    I am free;
I pay my company; it is my own;
I obey military orders.

DE GUICHE

      Oh!
That will be quite enough.
    (*To the Cadets*)
                    I can afford
Your little hates. My conduct under fire
Is well known. It was only yesterday
I drove the Count de Bucquoi from Bapaume,
Pouring my men down like an avalanche,
I myself led the charge—

CYRANO

    (*Without looking up from his book.*)
                    And your white scarf?

DE GUICHE

(*Surprised and gratified*)

You heard that episode? Yes—rallying
My men for the third time, I found myself
Carried among a crowd of fugitives
Into the enemy's lines. I was in danger
Of being shot or captured; but I thought
Quickly—took off and flung away the scarf
That marked my military rank—and so
Being inconspicuous, escaped among
My own force, rallied them, returned again
And won the day! . . .

> (*The Cadets do not appear to be listening, but here
> and there the cards and the dice boxes remain
> motionless, the smoke is retained in their
> cheeks.*)

What do you say to that?
Presence of mind—yes?

CYRANO

Henry of Navarre

Being outnumbered, never flung away
His white plume.

> (*Silent enjoyment. The cards flutter, the dice roll,
> the smoke puffs out.*)

DE GUICHE

My device was a success,

However!

> (*Same attentive pause, interrupting the games and
> the smoking.*)

CYRANO

Possibly . . . An officer
Does not lightly resign the privilege
Of being a target.

(*Cards, dice, and smoke fall, roll, and float away
with increasing satisfaction.*)

Now, if I had been there—
Your courage and my own differ in this—
When your scarf fell, I should have put it on.

DE GUICHE

Boasting again!

CYRANO

Boasting? Lend it to me
To-night; I'll lead the first charge, with your scarf
Over my shoulder!

DE GUICHE

Gasconnade once more!
You are safe making that offer, and you know it—
My scarf lies on the river bank between
The lines, a spot swept by artillery
Impossible to reach alive!

CYRANO

(*Produces the scarf from his pocket*)
Yes. Here . . .

(*Silence. The Cadets stifle their laughter behind
their cards and their dice boxes. DE GUICHE turns
to look at them. Immediately they resume their
gravity and their game. One of them whistles*)

*carelessly the mountain air which the fifer was
playing.*)

DE GUICHE

(*Takes the scarf.*)

Thank you! That bit of white is what I need
To make a signal. I was hesitating—
You have decided me.

(*He goes up to the parapet, climbs upon it, and
waves the scarf at arm's length several times.*)

ALL

What is he doing?—

What?—

THE SENTRY ON THE PARAPET

There's a man down there running away!

DE GUICHE

(*Descending*)

A Spaniard. Very useful as a spy
To both sides. He informs the enemy
As I instruct him. By his influence
I can arrange their dispositions.

CYRANO

Traitor!

DE GUICHE

(*Folding the scarf.*)

A traitor, yes; but useful . . .

We were saying? . . .

Oh, yes— Here is a bit of news for you:
Last night we had hopes of reprovisioning

The army. Under cover of the dark,
The Marshal moved to Dourlens. Our supplies
Are there. He may reach them. But to return
Safely, he needs a large force—at least half
Our entire strength. At present, we have here
Merely a skeleton.

CARBON

Fortunately,
The Spaniards do not know that.

DE GUICHE

Oh, yes; they know.
They will attack.

CARBON

Ah!

DE GUICHE

From that spy of mine
I learned of their intention. His report
Will determine the point of their advance.
The fellow asked me what to say! I told him:
"Go out between the lines; watch for my signal;
Where you see that, let them attack there."

CARBON

(*To the Cadets*)

Well,
Gentlemen!
      (*All rise. Noise of sword belts and breast-plates
      being buckled on.*)

DE GUICHE

You may have perhaps an hour.

FIRST CADET

Oh— An hour!
> (*They all sit down and resume their games once
> more.*)

DE GUICHE

(*To* CARBON)
                    The great thing is to gain time.
Any moment the Marshal may return.

CARBON

And to gain time?

DE GUICHE
                    You will all be so kind
As to lay down your lives!

CYRANO
                    Ah! Your revenge?

DE GUICHE

I make no great pretense of loving you!
But—since you gentlemen esteem yourselves
Invincible, the bravest of the brave,
And all that—why need we be personal?
I serve the king in choosing . . . as I choose!

CYRANO

(*Salutes*)
Sir, permit me to offer—all our thanks.

DE GUICHE

(*Returns the salute.*)
You love to fight a hundred against one;

Here is your opportunity!
        (*He goes up stage with* CARBON)

                    CYRANO
    (*To the Cadets*)
                        My friends,
We shall add now to our old Gascon arms
With their six chevrons, blue and gold, a seventh—
Blood-red!
        (DE GUICHE *talks in a low tone to* CARBON *up stage.*
        Orders are given. The defense is arranged. CY-
        RANO *goes to* CHRISTIAN, *who has remained mo-*
        tionless with folded arms.)
            Christian?
    (*Lays a hand on his shoulder.*)

                CHRISTIAN
    (*Shakes his head.*)
                Roxane . . .

                CYRANO
                            Yes.

                CHRISTIAN
                            I should like
To say farewell to her, with my whole heart
Written for her to keep.

                CYRANO
                I thought of that—
    (*Takes a letter from his doublet.*)
I have written your farewell.
                CHRISTIAN
                    Show me!

CYRANO

You wish

To read it?

CHRISTIAN

Of course!
(*He takes the letter; begins to read, looks up suddenly.*)

What?—

CYRANO

What is it?

CHRISTIAN

Look—

This little circle—

CYRANO

(*Takes back the letter quickly, and looks innocent.*)
Circle?—

CHRISTIAN

Yes—a tear!

CYRANO

So it is! . . . Well—a poet while he writes
Is like a lover in his lady's arms,
Believing his imagination—all
Seems true—you understand? There's half the charm
Of writing— Now, this letter as you see
I have made so pathetic that I wept
While I was writing it!

CHRISTIAN

You—wept?

CYRANO

Why, yes—

Because . . . it is a little thing to die,
But—not to see her . . . that is terrible!
And I shall never—

(CHRISTIAN *looks at him.*)

We shall never—

(*Quickly*)

You

Will never—

CHRISTIAN

(*Snatches the letter.*)

Give me that!
(*Noise in the distance on the outskirts of the camp*)

VOICE OF A SENTRY

Halt—who goes there?

(*Shots, shouting, jingle of harness*)

CARBON

What is it?—

THE SENTRY ON THE PARAPET

Why, a coach.

(*They rush to look.*)

CONFUSED VOICES

What? In the Camp?

A coach? Coming this way— It must have driven
Through the Spanish lines—what the devil— Fire!—
No— Hark! The driver shouting—what does he say?
Wait— He said: "On the service of the King!"

*(They are all on the parapet looking over. The
jingling comes nearer.)*

DE GUICHE

Of the King?
(They come down and fall into line.)

CARBON

Hats off, all!

DE GUICHE

(Speaks off stage.)

The King! Fall in,

Rascals!—
*(The coach enters at full trot. It is covered with
mud and dust. The curtains are drawn. Two footmen are seated behind. It stops suddenly.)*

CARBON

(Shouts)

Beat the assembly—
(Roll of drums. All the Cadets uncover.)

DE GUICHE

Lower the steps—open the door—
(Two men rush to the coach. The door opens.)

ROXANE

(Comes out of the coach.)

Good morning!
*(At the sound of a woman's voice, every head is
raised. Sensation.)*

DE GUICHE

On the King's service— You?

ROXANE

Yes—my own king—

Love!

CYRANO

(*Aside*)
God is merciful . . .

CHRISTIAN

(*Hastens to her.*)

You! Why have you—

ROXANE

Your war lasted so long!

CHRISTIAN

But why?—

ROXANE

Not now—

CYRANO

(*Aside*)
I wonder if I dare to look at her . . .

DE GUICHE

You cannot remain here!

ROXANE

Why, certainly!
Roll that drum here, somebody . . .
(*She sits on the drum, which is brought to her.*)

Thank you— There!
(*She laughs.*)
Would you believe—they fired upon us?

—My coach

Looks like the pumpkin in the fairy tale,
Does it not? And my footmen—

>   (*She throws a kiss to* CHRISTIAN.)

>   How do you do?

>   (*She looks about.*)

How serious you all are! Do you know,
It is a long drive here—from Arras?

>   (*Sees* CYRANO.)

>   Cousin,

I am glad to see you!

CYRANO

>   (*Advances*)

>   Oh— How did you come?

ROXANE

How did I find you? Very easily—
I followed where the country was laid waste
—Oh, but I saw such things! I had to see
To believe. Gentlemen, is that the service
Of your King? I prefer my own!

CYRANO

>   But how

Did you come through?

ROXANE

>   Why, through the Spanish lines

Of course!

FIRST CADET

They let you pass?—

DE GUICHE

What did you say?
How did you manage?

LE BRET

Yes, that must have been
Difficult!

ROXANE

No— I simply drove along.
Now and then some hidalgo scowled at me
And I smiled back—my best smile; whereupon,
The Spaniards being (without prejudice
To the French) the most polished gentlemen
In the world—I passed!

CARBON

Certainly that smile
Should be a passport! Did they never ask
Your errand or your destination?

ROXANE

Oh,
Frequently! Then I drooped my eyes and said:
"I have a lover . . ." Whereupon, the Spaniard
With an air of ferocious dignity
Would close the carriage door—with such a gesture
As any king might envy, wave aside
The muskets that were levelled at my breast,
Fall back three paces, equally superb
In grace and gloom, draw himself up, thrust forth
A spur under his cloak, sweeping the air

With his long plumes, bow very low, and say:
"Pass, Señorita!"

CHRISTIAN

But, Roxane—

ROXANE

I know-
I said "a lover"—but you understand—
Forgive me!—If I said "I am going to meet
My husband," no one would believe me!

CHRISTIAN

Yes,

But—

ROXANE

What then?

DE GUICHE

You must leave this place.

CYRANO

At once.

ROXANE

I?

LE BRET

Yes—immediately.

ROXANE

And why?

CHRISTIAN

(*Embarrassed*)

Because . . .

CYRANO

(Same)

In half an hour . . .

DE GUICHE

(Same)

Or three quarters . . .

CARBON

(Same)

Perhaps

It might be better . . .

LE BRET

If you . . .

ROXANE

Oh— I see!

You are going to fight. I remain here.

ALL

No—no!

ROXANE

He is my husband—

(Throws herself in CHRISTIAN's arms.)

I will die with you!

CHRISTIAN

Your eyes! . . . Why do you?—

ROXANE

You know why . . .

DE GUICHE

(Desperate)

This post

Is dangerous—

ROXANE

(*Turns*)

How—dangerous?

CYRANO

The proof

Is, we are ordered—

ROXANE

(*To* De Guiche)

Oh—you wish to make

A widow of me?

DE GUICHE

On my word of honor—

ROXANE

No matter. I am just a little mad—
I will stay. It may be amusing.

CYRANO

What,

A heroine—our intellectual?

ROXANE

Monsieur de Bergerac, I am your cousin!

A CADET

We'll fight now! Hurrah!

ROXANE

(*More and more excited*)

I am safe with you—my friends!

ANOTHER

(*Carried away*)
The whole camp breathes of lilies!—

ROXANE

　　　　　　　　　　　And I think,
This hat would look well on the battlefield! . . .
But perhaps—

　　　(*Looks at* De Guiche.)

　　　　　　　The Count ought to leave us. Any moment
Now, there may be danger.

DE GUICHE

　　　　　　　　　　This is too much!
I must inspect my guns. I shall return—
You may change your mind— There will yet be time—

ROXANE

Never!

　　　(De Guiche *goes out.*)

CHRISTIAN

　　　(*Imploring*)
　　　　Roxane! . . .

ROXANE

　　　　No!

FIRST CADET

(*To the rest*)

　　　　　　　　　　She stays here!

ALL

(*Rushing about, elbowing each other, brushing off
　　their clothes.*)

　　　　　　　　　　　　　　　A comb!—
Soap!—Here's a hole in my— A needle!—Who
Has a ribbon?—Your mirror, quick!—My cuffs—
A razor—

ROXANE

(To CYRANO, *who is still urging her***)**
No! I shall not stir one step!

CARBON

(*Having, like the others, tightened his belt, dusted himself, brushed off his hat, smoothed out his plume and put on his lace cuffs, advances to* ROXANE *ceremoniously.***)**
In that case, may I not present to you
Some of these gentlemen who are to have
The honor of dying in your presence?

ROXANE

(*Bows***)**

Please!—
(*She waits, standing, on the arm of* CHRISTIAN, *while*

CARBON

(*—presents***)**
Baron de Peyrescous de Colignac!

THE CADET

(*Salutes***)**
Madame . . .

ROXANE

Monsieur . . .

CARBON

(*Continues***)**

Baron de Casterac
De Cahuzac— Vidame de Malgouyre
Estressac Lésbas d'Escarabiot—

THE VIDAME

Madame . . .

CARBON

Chevalier d'Antignac-Juzet—
Baron Hillot de Blagnac-Saléchan
De Castel-Crabioules—

THE BARON

Madame . . .

ROXANE

How many
Names you all have!

THE BARON

Hundreds!

CARBON

(*To* ROXANE)

Open the hand
That holds your handkerchief.

ROXANE

(*Opens her hand; the handkerchief falls.*)
Why?
(*The whole company makes a movement toward
    it.*)

CARBON

(*Picks it up quickly.*)

My company
Was in want of a banner. We have now
The fairest in the army!

ROXANE

(*Smiling*)

Rather small—

CARBON

(*Fastens the handkerchief to his lance.*)

Lace—and embroidered!

A CADET

(*To the others*)

With her smiling on me,
I could die happy, if I only had
Something in my—

CARBON

(*Turns upon him*)

Shame on you! Feast your eyes
And forget your—

ROXANE

(*Quickly*)

It must be this fresh air—
I am starving! Let me see . . .

Cold partridges,
Pastry, a little white wine—that would do.
Will someone bring that to me?

A CADET

(*Aside*)

Will someone!—

ANOTHER

Where the devil are we to find—

ROXANE

(*Overhears; sweetly*)

Why, there—

In my carriage.

ALL

Wha-at?

ROXANE

All you have to **do**

Is to unpack, and carve, and serve things.

Oh,

Notice my coachman; you may recognize
An old friend.

THE CADETS

(*Rush to the coach.*)

Ragueneau!

ROXANE

(*Follows them with her eyes.*)

Poor fellows . . .

THE CADETS

(*Acclamations*)

Ah!

Ah!

CYRANO

(*Kisses her hand.*)

Our good fairy!

RAGUENEAU

(*Standing on his box, like a mountebank before
a crowd.*)

Gentlemen!—

(*Enthusiasm*)

THE CADETS

Bravo!

Bravo!

RAGUENEAU

The Spaniards, basking in our smiles,
Smiled on our baskets!

(*Applause*)

CYRANO

(*Aside, to* CHRISTIAN)

Christian!—

RAGUENEAU

They adored

The Fair, and missed—

(*He takes from under the seat a dish, which he
holds aloft.*)

the Fowl!

(*Applause. The dish is passed from hand to hand.*)

CYRANO

(*As before, to* CHRISTIAN)

One moment—

RAGUENEAU

Venus

Charmed their eyes while Adonis quietly

(*Brandishing a ham.*)

Brought home the Boar!

(*Applause; the ham is seized by a score of hands
outstretched.*)

CYRANO

(*As before.*)

Pst— Let me speak to you—

ROXANE

(*As the Cadets return, their arms full of provisions*)
Spread them out on the ground.
(*Calls*)

Christian! Come here;
Make yourself useful.

(CHRISTIAN *turns to her, at the moment when*
CYRANO *was leading him aside. She arranges
the food, with his aid and that of the two im-
perturbable footmen.*)

RAGUENEAU

Peacock, *aux truffes!*

FIRST CADET

(*Comes down, cutting a huge slice of the ham.*)

Tonnerre!
We are not going to die without a gorge—
(*Sees* ROXANE; *corrects himself hastily.*)
Pardon—a banquet!

RAGUENEAU

(*Tossing out the cushions of the carriage.*)

Open these—they are full
Of ortolans!
(*Tumult; laughter; the cushions are eviscerated.*)

THIRD CADET

Lucullus!

RAGUENEAU

(*Throws out bottles of red wine.*)
                              Flasks of ruby—
(*And of white*)
Flasks of topaz—

ROXANE

(*Throws a tablecloth at the head of* CYRANO.)
                    Come back out of your dreams!
Unfold this cloth—

RAGUENEAU

(*Takes off one of the lanterns of the carriage, and
    flourishes it.*)
                    Our lamps are bonbonnières!

CYRANO

(*To* CHRISTIAN)
I must see you before you speak with her—

RAGUENEAU

(*More and more lyrical*)
My whip-handle is one long sausage!

ROXANE

(*Pouring wine; passing the food.*)
                              We
Being about to die, first let us dine!
Never mind the others—all for Gascoyne!
And if de Guiche comes, he is not invited!
        (*Going from one to another.*)
Plenty of time—you need not eat so fast—
Hold your cup—

(*To another*)

What's the matter?

THE CADET

(*Sobbing*)

You are so good

To us . . .

ROXANE

There, there! Red or white wine?

—Some bread

For Monsieur de Carbon!—Napkins— A knife—
Pass your plate— Some of the crust? A little more—
Light or dark?—Burgundy?—

CYRANO

(*Follows her with an armful of dishes, helping to
serve.*)

Adorable!

ROXANE

(*Goes to* CHRISTIAN.)

What would you like?

CHRISTIAN

Nothing.

ROXANE

Oh, but you must!—

A little wine? A biscuit?

CHRISTIAN

Tell me first

Why you came—

ROXANE

By and by. I must take care
Of these poor boys—

LE BRET

(*Who has gone up stage to pass up food to the
sentry on the parapet, on the end of a lance.*)
De Guiche!

CYRANO

Hide everything

Quick!—Dishes, bottles, tablecloth—

Now look

Hungry again—
(*To* RAGUENEAU)

You there! Up on your box—
—Everything out of sight?—
(*In a twinkling, everything has been pushed inside
the tents, hidden in their hats or under their
cloaks. DE GUICHE enters quickly, then stops,
sniffing the air. Silence.*)

DE GUICHE

It smells good here.

A CADET

(*Humming with an air of great unconcern.*)
Sing ha-ha-ha and ho-ho-ho—

DE GUICHE

(*Stares at him; he grows embarrassed.*)

You there—

What are you blushing for?

THE CADET

Nothing—my blood
Stirs at the thought of battle.

ANOTHER

Pom . . . pom . . . pom! . . .

DE GUICHE

(*Turns upon him.*)
What is that?

THE CADET

(*Slightly stimulated*)
Only song—only little song—　　..

DE GUICHE

You appear happy!

THE CADET

Oh, yes—always happy
Before a fight—

DE GUICHE

(*Calls to* CARBON, *for the purpose of giving him
an order.*)
Captain! I—
(*Stops and looks at him.*)
What the devil—
You are looking happy too!—

CARBON

(*Pulls a long face and hides a bottle behind his
back.*)
No!

DE GUICHE

Here—I had

One gun remaining. I have had it placed
(*He points off stage.*)
There—in that corner—for your men.

A CADET

(*Simpering*)

So kind!—

Charming attention!

ANOTHER

(*Same business; burlesque*)

Sweet solicitude!—

DE GUICHE

(*Contemptuous*)

I believe you are both drunk—
(*Coldly*)

Being unaccustomed

To guns—take care of the recoil!

FIRST CADET

(*Gesture*)

Ah-h . . . Pfft!

DE GUICHE

(*Goes up to him, furious.*)

How dare you?

FIRST CADET

A Gascon's gun never recoils!

DE GUICHE

(*Shakes him by the arm.*)

You *are* drunk—

FIRST CADET

(Superbly)

With the smell of powder!

DE GUICHE

(Turns away with a shrug.)

Bah!

(To ROXANE*)*

Madame, have you decided?

ROXANE

I stay here.

DE GUICHE

You have time to escape—

ROXANE

No!

DE GUICHE

Very well—

Someone give me a musket!

CARBON

What!

DE GUICHE

I stay

Here also.

CYRANO

(Formally)

Sir, you show courage!

FIRST CADET

A Gascon

In spite of all that lace!

ROXANE
Why—

DE GUICHE

Must I run

Away, and leave a woman?

SECOND CADET

(*To First Cadet*)

We might give him

Something to eat—what do you say?
(*All the food reappears, as if by magic.*)

DE GUICHE
(*His face lights up.*)

A feast!

THIRD CADET
Here a little, there a little—

DE GUICHE
(*Recovers his self-control; haughtily.*)

Do you think

I want your leavings?

CYRANO

(*Saluting*)

Colonel—you improve!

DE GUICHE

I can fight as I am!

FIRST CADET

(*Delighted*)

Listen to him—

He has an accent!

DE GUICHE

(*Laughs*)

Have I so?

FIRST CADET

A Gascon!—

A Gascon, after all!

(*They all begin to dance.*)

CARBON

(*Who has disappeared for a moment behind the parapet, reappears on top of it.*)

I have placed my pikemen

Here.

(*Indicates a row of pikes showing above the parapet.*)

DE GUICHE

(*Bows to* ROXANE.)

We'll review them; will you take my arm?

(*She takes his arm; they go up on the parapet. The rest uncover, and follow them up stage.*)

CHRISTIAN

(*Goes hurriedly to* CYRANO.)

Speak quickly!

(*At the moment when* ROXANE *appears on the parapet the pikes are lowered in salute, and a cheer is heard. She bows.*)

THE PIKEMEN

(*Off stage*)

Hurrah!

CHRISTIAN

What is it?

CYRANO

If Roxane . . .

CHRISTIAN

Well?

CYRANO

Speaks about your letters . . .

CHRISTIAN

Yes—I know!

CYRANO

Do not make the mistake of showing . . .

CHRISTIAN

What?

CYRANO

Showing surprise.

CHRISTIAN

Surprise—why?

CYRANO

I must tell you! . . .
It is quite simple—I had forgotten it
Until just now. You have . . .

CHRISTIAN

Speak quickly!

CYRANO

You

Have written oftener than you think.

CHRISTIAN

Oh—have I!

CYRANO

I took upon me to interpret you;
And wrote—sometimes . . . without . . .

CHRISTIAN

My knowing. Well?

CYRANO

Perfectly simple!

CHRISTIAN

Oh, yes, perfectly!—
For a month, we have been blockaded here!—
How did you send all these letters?

CYRANO

Before

Daylight, I managed—

CHRISTIAN

I see. That was also

Perfectly simple!

—So I wrote to her,
How many times a week? Twice? Three times?
   Four?

CYRANO

Oftener.

CHRISTIAN

Every day?

CYRANO

Yes—every day . . .
Every single day . . .

CHRISTIAN

(Violently)

And that wrought you up
Into such a flame that you faced death—

CYRANO

(Sees ROXANE *returning.)*

Hush—

Not before her!

(He goes quickly into the tent. ROXANE *comes up
to* CHRISTIAN.*)*

ROXANE

Now—Christian!

CHRISTIAN

(Takes her hands.)

Tell me now
Why you came here—over these ruined roads—
Why you made your way among mosstroopers
And ruffians—you—to join me here?

ROXANE

Because—

Your letters . . .

CHRISTIAN

Meaning?

ROXANE

It was your own fault
If I ran into danger! I went mad—
Mad with you! Think what you have written me,
How many times, each one more wonderful
Than the last!

CHRISTIAN
All this for a few absurd

Love-letters—

ROXANE
Hush—absurd! How can you **know?**
I thought I loved you, ever since one night
When a voice that I never would have known
Under my window breathed your soul to me . . .
But—all this time, your letters—every one
Was like hearing your voice there in the dark,
All around me, like your arms around me . . .
   (*More lightly*)

                                             At last,

I came. Anyone would! Do you suppose
The prim Penelope had stayed at home
Embroidering,—if Ulysses wrote like you?
She would have fallen like another Helen—
Tucked up those linen petticoats of hers
And followed him to Troy!

CHRISTIAN
                    But you—

ROXANE
                                   I read them
Over and over. I grew faint reading them.
I belonged to you. Every page of them
Was like a petal fallen from your soul—
Like the light and the fire of a great love,
Sweet and strong and true—

CHRISTIAN

Sweet . . . and strong . . . and true . . .
You felt that, Roxane?—

ROXANE

You know how I feel! . . .

CHRISTIAN

So—you came . . .

ROXANE

Oh, my Christian, oh my king,—
Lift me up if I fall upon my knees—
It is the heart of me that kneels to you,
And will remain forever at your feet—
You cannot lift that!—

I came here to say
'Forgive me'—(It is time to be forgiven
Now, when we may die presently)—forgive me
For being light and vain and loving you
Only because you were beautiful.

CHRISTIAN

(*Astonished*)

Roxane! . . .

ROXANE

Afterwards I knew better. Afterwards
(I had to learn to use my wings) I loved you
For yourself too—knowing you more, and loving
More of you. And now—

CHRISTIAN

Now? . . .

ROXANE

It is yourself
I love now: your own self.

CHRISTIAN

(*Taken aback*)

Roxane!

ROXANE

(*Gravely*)

Be happy!—
You must have suffered; for you must have seen
How frivolous I was; and to be loved
For the mere costume, the poor casual body
You went about in—to a soul like yours,
That must have been torture! Therefore with words
You revealed your heart. Now that image of you
Which filled my eyes first—I see better now,
And I see it no more!

CHRISTIAN

Oh!—

ROXANE

You still doubt
Your victory?

CHRISTIAN

(*Miserably*)

Roxane!—

ROXANE

I understand:
You cannot perfectly believe in me—
A love like this—

CHRISTIAN

I want no love like this!
I want love only for—

ROXANE

Only for what
Every woman sees in you? I can do
Better than that!

CHRISTIAN

No—it was best before!

ROXANE

You do not altogether know me . . . Dear,
There is more of me than there was—with this,
I can love more of you—more of what makes
You your own self—Truly! . . . If you were less
Lovable—

CHRISTIAN

No!

ROXANE

—Less charming—ugly even—
I should love you still.

CHRISTIAN

You mean that?

ROXANE

I do
Mean that!

CHRISTIAN

Ugly? . . .

ROXANE

Yes. Even then!

CHRISTIAN

(*Agonized*)

Oh . . . God! . . .

ROXANE

Now are you happy?

CHRISTIAN

(*Choking*)

Yes . . .

ROXANE

What is it?

CHRISTIAN

(*Pushes her away gently.*)

Only . . .

Nothing . . . one moment . . .

ROXANE

But—

CHRISTIAN

(*Gesture toward* THE CADETS)

I am keeping you

From those poor fellows— Go and smile at them;
They are going to die!

ROXANE

(*Softly*)

Dear Christian!

CHRISTIAN

Go—

(*She goes up among the Gascons, who gather
round her respectfully.*)

Cyrano!

CYRANO
(Comes out of the tent, armed for the battle.)
What is wrong? You look—

CHRISTIAN
She does not

Love me any more.

CYRANO
(Smiles)
You think not?

CHRISTIAN
She loves

You.

CYRANO
No!—

CHRISTIAN
(Bitterly)
She loves only my soul.

CYRANO
No!

CHRISTIAN
Yes—

That means you. And you love her.

CYRANO
I?

CHRISTIAN
I see—

I know!

CYRANO
That is true . . .

CHRISTIAN

More than—

CYRANO

(Quietly)

More than that.

CHRISTIAN

Tell her so!

CYRANO

No.

CHRISTIAN

Why not?

CYRANO

Why—look at me!

CHRISTIAN

She would love me if I were ugly.

CYRANO

(Startled)

She—

Said that?

CHRISTIAN

Yes. Now then!

CYRANO

(Half to himself)

It was good of her

To tell you that . . .

(Change of tone)

Nonsense! Do not believe

Any such madness—

It was good of her

To tell you . . .
                    Do not take her at her word!
Go on—you never will be ugly— Go!
She would never forgive me.

CHRISTIAN
                        That is what
We shall see.

CYRANO
        No, no—

CHRISTIAN
                    Let her choose between us!—
Tell her everything!

CYRANO
                No—you torture me—

CHRISTIAN
Shall I ruin your happiness, because
I have a cursed pretty face? That seems
Too unfair!

CYRANO
            And am I to ruin yours
Because I happen to be born with power
To say what you—perhaps—feel?

CHRISTIAN
                            Tell her!

CYRANO
                                Man—
Do not try me too far!

CHRISTIAN
                    I am tired of being
My own rival!

CYRANO
            Christian!—

CHRISTIAN
                            Our secret marriage—
No witnesses—fraudulent—that can be
Annulled—

CYRANO
            Do not try me—

CHRISTIAN
                            I want her love
For the poor fool I am—or not at all!
Oh, I am going through with this! I'll know,
One way or the other. Now I shall walk down
To the end of the post. Go tell her. Let her choose
One of us.

CYRANO
            It will be you.

CHRISTIAN
                        God—I hope so!
    (*He turns and calls.*)
Roxane!

CYRANO
            No—no—

ROXANE
    (*Hurries down to him.*)
                    Yes, Christian?

CHRISTIAN

Cyrano

Has news for you—important.
    (*She turns to* CYRANO. CHRISTIAN *goes out.*)

ROXANE

(*Lightly*)

Oh—important?

CYRANO

He is gone . . .
    (*To* ROXANE)

Nothing—only Christian thinks
You ought to know—

ROXANE

I do know. He still doubts
What I told him just now. I saw that.

CYRANO

(*Takes her hand.*)

Was it
True—what you told him just now?

ROXANE

It was true!
I said that I should love him even . . .

CYRANO

(*Smiling sadly*)

The word
Comes hard—before me?

ROXANE

Even if he were . . .

CYRANO

Say it—

I shall not be hurt!—Ugly?

ROXANE
Even then

I should love him.

(A few shots, off stage, in the direction in which
CHRISTIAN *disappeared.)*
Hark! The guns—

CYRANO

Hideous?

ROXANE

Hideous.

CYRANO

Disfigured?

ROXANE
Or disfigured.

CYRANO

Even

Grotesque?

ROXANE
How could he ever be grotesque—
Ever—to me!

CYRANO
But you could love him so,
As much as?—

ROXANE
Yes—and more!

CYRANO

(*Aside, excitedly*)

It is true!—true!—
Perhaps—God! This is too much happiness . . .
        (*To* ROXANE)
I—Roxane—listen—

LE BRET

(*Enters quickly; calls to* CYRANO *in a low tone.*)
        Cyrano—

CYRANO

(*Turns*)

Yes?

LE BRET

Hush! . . .

(*Whispers a few words to him.*)

CYRANO

(*Lets fall* ROXANE'S *hand.*)

Ah!

ROXANE

What is it?

CYRANO

(*Half stunned, and aside*)
        All gone . . .

ROXANE

(*More shots*)

What is it? **Oh,**

They are fighting!—
        (*She goes up to look off stage.*)

CYRANO

All gone. I cannot ever
Tell her, now . . . ever . . .

ROXANE

(*Starts to rush away.*)

What has happened?

CYRANO

(*Restrains her.*)

Nothing.
(*Several Cadets enter. They conceal something
which they are carrying, and form a group so as
to prevent* ROXANE *from seeing their burden.*)

ROXANE

These men—

CYRANO

Come away . . .
(*He leads her away from the group.*)

ROXANE

You were telling me
Something—

CYRANO

Oh, that? Nothing . . .
(*Gravely*)

I swear to you
That the spirit of Christian—that his soul
Was—
(*Corrects himself quickly.*)
That his soul is no less great—

ROXANE

(*Catches at the word.*)

Was?

(*Crying out*)

Oh!—

(*She rushes among the men, and scatters them.*)

CYRANO

All gone . . .

ROXANE

(*Sees* CHRISTIAN *lying upon his cloak.*)
Christian!

LE BRET

(*To* CYRANO)

At the first volley.

(ROXANE *throws herself upon the body of* CHRIS-
TIAN. *Shots; at first scattered, then increasing.
Drums. Voices shouting.*)

CARBON

(*Sword in hand*)

Here

They come!—Ready!—

(*Followed by the Cadets, he climbs over the parapet and disappears.*)

ROXANE

Christian!

CARBON

(*Off stage*)

Come on, there, You!

ROXANE

Christian!

CARBON

Fall in!

ROXANE

Christian!

CARBON

Measure your fuse!

(RAGUENEAU *hurries up, carrying a helmet full of water.*)

CHRISTIAN

(*Faintly*)

Roxane! . . .

CYRANO

(*Low and quick, in* CHRISTIAN'S *ear, while* ROXANE *is dipping into the water a strip of linen torn from her dress.*)

I have told her; she loves you.

(CHRISTIAN *closes his eyes.*)

ROXANE

(*Turns to* CHRISTIAN.)

Yes,

My darling?

CARBON

Draw your ramrods!

ROXANE

(*To* CYRANO)

He is not dead? . . .

CARBON

Open your charges!

ROXANE

I can feel his cheek
Growing cold against mine—

* CARBON

Take aim!

ROXANE

A letter–

Over his heart—
(*She opens it.*)
For me.

CYRANO

(*Aside*)

My letter . . .

CARBON

Fire!
(*Musketry, cries and groans. Din of battle.*)

CYRANO

(*Trying to withdraw his hand, which* ROXANE,
still upon her knees, is holding.)
But, Roxane—they are fighting—

ROXANE

Wait a little . . .

He is dead. No one else knew him but you . . .
(*She weeps quietly.*)
Was he not a great lover, a great man,
A hero?

CYRANO

(*Standing, bareheaded.*)
Yes, Roxane.

ROXANE

A poet, unknown,
Adorable?

CYRANO

Yes, Roxane.

ROXANE

A fine mind?

CYRANO

Yes, Roxane.

ROXANE

A heart deeper than we knew—
A soul magnificently tender?

CYRANO

(*Firmly*)

Yes,
Roxane!

ROXANE

(*Sinks down upon the breast of* CHRISTIAN.)
He is dead now . . .

CYRANO

(*Aside; draws his sword.*)

Why, so am I—
For I am dead, and my love mourns for me
And does not know . . .

(*Trumpets in distance*)

DE GUICHE

(*Appears on the parapet, disheveled, wounded on the forehead, shouting.*)

The signal—hark—the trumpets! The army has returned— Hold them now!—Hold them! The army!—

ROXANE

On his letter—blood . . . and tears.

A VOICE

(*Off stage*)

Surrender!

THE CADETS

No!

RAGUENEAU

This place is dangerous!—

CYRANO

(*To* DE GUICHE)

Take her away—I am going—

ROXANE

(*Kisses the letter; faintly.*)

His blood . . . his tears . . .

RAGUENEAU

(*Leaps down from the coach and runs to her.*)

She has fainted—

DE GUICHE

(*On the parapet; savagely, to the Cadets*)

Hold them!

VOICE OFF STAGE

Lay down your arms!

VOICES

No! No!

CYRANO

(To DE GUICHE*)*
Sir, you have proved yourself— Take care of her.

DE GUICHE

(Hurries to ROXANE *and takes her up in his arms.)*
As you will—we can win, if you hold on
A little longer—

CYRANO

Good!
(Calls out to ROXANE, *as she is carried away, fainting, by* DE GUICHE *and* RAGUENEAU.*)*
Adieu, Roxane!
*(Tumult, outcries. Several Cadets come back
wounded and fall on the stage.* CYRANO, *rushing
to the fight, is stopped on the crest of the parapet
by* CARBON, *covered with blood.)*

CARBON

We are breaking—I am twice wounded—

CYRANO

(Shouts to the Gascons.)

Hardi!

Reculez pas, Drollos!
(To CARBON, *holding him up.)*
So—never fear!
I have two deaths to avenge now—Christian's
And my own!

(They come down. CYRANO *takes from him the lance with* ROXANE's *handkerchief still fastened to it.)*

Float, little banner, with her name!

(He plants it on the parapet; then shouts to The Cadets.)

Toumbé dessus! Escrasas lous!

(To the fifer)

Your fife!

Music!

(Fife plays. The wounded drag themselves to their feet. Other Cadets scramble over the parapet and group themselves around CYRANO *and his tiny flag. The coach is filled and covered with men, bristling with muskets, transformed into a redoubt.)*

A CADET

(Reels backward over the wall, still fighting, shouts.)

They are climbing over!—

(And falls dead.)

CYRANO

Very good—

Let them come!— A salute now—

(The parapet is crowned for an instant with a rank of enemies. The imperial banner of Spain is raised aloft.)

Fire!

(General volley)

VOICE
(Among the ranks of the enemy)

Fire!

(Murderous counter-fire; the Cadets fall on every side.)

A SPANISH OFFICER
(Uncovers)

Who are these men who are so fond of death?

CYRANO
(Erect amid the hail of bullets, declaims.)
The Cadets of Gascoyne, the defenders
Of Carbon de Castel-Jaloux—
Free fighters, free lovers, free spenders—
(He rushes forward, followed by a few survivors.)
The Cadets of Cascoyne . . .
(The rest is lost in the din of battle.)

(Curtain)

THE FIFTH ACT
CYRANO'S GAZETTE

Fifteen years later, in 1655. THE PARK OF THE CONVENT *occupied by the Ladies of the Cross, at Paris.*

Magnificent foliage. To the Left, the House upon a broad Terrace at the head of a flight of steps, with several Doors opening upon the Terrace. In the centre of the scene an enormous Tree alone in the centre of a little open space. Toward the Right, in the foreground, among Boxwood Bushes, a semicircular Bench of stone.

All the way across the Background of the scene, an Avenue overarched by the chestnut trees, leading to the door of a Chapel on the Right, just visible among the branches of the trees. Beyond the double curtain of the trees, we catch a glimpse of bright lawns and shaded walks, masses of shrubbery; the perspective of the Park; the sky.

A little side door of the Chapel opens upon a Colonnade, garlanded with Autumnal vines, and disappearing on the Right behind the box-trees.

It is late October. Above the still living green of the turf all the foliage is red and yellow and brown. The evergreen masses of Box and Yew stand out darkly against this Autumnal coloring. A heap of dead leaves under every tree. The leaves are falling everywhere. They rustle underfoot along the walks; the Terrace and the Bench are half covered with them.

Before the Bench on the Right, on the side toward the Tree, is placed a tall embroidery frame and beside it a little Chair. Baskets filled with skeins of many-colored silks and balls of wool. Tapestry unfinished on the Frame.

At the CURTAIN RISE *the nuns are coming and going across the Park; several of them are seated on the Bench around* MOTHER MARGUÉRITE DE JÉSUS. *The leaves are falling.*

SISTER MARTHE

(*To* MOTHER MARGUÉRITE)

Sister Claire has been looking in the glass
At her new cap; twice!

MOTHER MARGUÉRITE

(*To* SISTER CLAIRE)

It is very plain;
Very.

SISTER CLAIRE

And Sister Marthe stole a plum
Out of the tart this morning!

MOTHER MARGUÉRITE

(*To* SISTER MARTHE)

That was wrong;
Very wrong.

SISTER CLAIRE

Oh, but such a little look!

SISTER MARTHE

Such a little plum!

MOTHER MARGUÉRITE

(*Severely*)

I shall tell Monsieur
De Cyrano, this evening.

SISTER CLAIRE

No! Oh no!—
He will make fun of us.

SISTER MARTHE

He will say nuns
Are so gay!

SISTER CLAIRE

And so greedy!

MOTHER MARGUÉRITE

(*Smiling*)

And so good . . .

SISTER CLAIRE

It must be ten years, Mother Marguérite,
That he has come here every Saturday,
Is it not?

MOTHER MARGUÉRITE

More than ten years; ever since
His cousin came to live among us here—
Her worldly weeds among our linen veils,
Her widowhood and our virginity—
Like a black dove among white doves.

SISTER MARTHE

No one
Else ever turns that happy sorrow of hers
Into a smile.

ALL THE NUNS

He is such fun!—He makes us
Almost laugh!—And he teases everyone—
And pleases everyone— And we all love him—
And he likes our cake, too—

SISTER MARTHE

I am afraid
He is not a good Catholic.

SISTER CLAIRE

Some day
We shall convert him.

THE NUNS

Yes—yes!

MOTHER MARGUÉRITE

Let him be;
I forbid you to worry him. Perhaps
He might stop coming here.

SISTER MARTHE

But . . . God?

MOTHER MARGUÉRITE

You need not
Be afraid. God knows all about him.

SISTER MARTHE

Yes . . .
But every Saturday he says to me,
Just as if he were proud of it, "Well, Sister,
I ate meat yesterday!"

MOTHER MARGUÉRITE

He tells you so?
The last time he said that, he had not eaten
Anything for two days.

SISTER MARTHE

Mother!—

MOTHER MARGUÉRITE

He is poor;

Very poor.

SISTER MARTHE

Who said so?

MOTHER MARGUÉRITE

Monsieur Le Bret.

SISTER MARTHE

Why does not someone help him?

MOTHER MARGUÉRITE

He would be

Angry; very angry . . .
(*Between the trees up stage,* ROXANE *appears, all in
black, with a widow's cap and long veils. DE
GUICHE, magnificently grown old, walks beside
her. They move slowly.* MOTHER MARGUÉRITE
rises.)

Let us go in—
Madame Madeleine has a visitor.

SISTER MARTHE

(*To* SISTER CLAIRE)
The Duc de Grammont, is it not? The Marshal?

SISTER CLAIRE

(*Looks toward* De Guiche.)

I think so—yes.

SISTER MARTHE

He has not been to see her

For months—

THE NUNS

He is busy—the Court!—The Camp!—

SISTER CLAIRE

The world . . .

(*They go out.* De Guiche *and* Roxane *come down in silence, and stop near the embroidery frame. Pause.*)

DE GUICHE

And you remain here, wasting all that gold—
For ever in mourning?

ROXANE

For ever.

DE GUICHE

And still faithful?

ROXANE

And still faithful . . .

DE GUICHE

(*After a pause*)

Have you forgiven me?

ROXANE

(*Simply, looking up at the cross of the Convent*)

I am here.

(*Another pause*)

DE GUICHE

Was Christian . . . all that?

ROXANE

If you knew him.

DE GUICHE

Ah? We were not precisely . . . intimate . . .
And his last letter—always at your heart?

ROXANE

It hangs here, like a holy reliquary.

DE GUICHE

Dead—and you love him still!

ROXANE

Sometimes I think

He has not altogether died; our hearts
Meet, and his love flows all around me, living.

DE GUICHE

(*After another pause*)
You see Cyrano often?

ROXANE

Every week.

My old friend takes the place of my Gazette,
Brings me all the news. Every Saturday,
Under that tree where you are now, his chair
Stands, if the day be fine. I wait for him,
Embroidering; the hour strikes; then I hear,
(I need not turn to look!) at the last stroke,
His cane tapping the steps. He laughs at me

For my eternal needlework. He tells
The story of the past week—

    (Le Bret *appears on the steps.*)

                There's Le Bret!—

    (Le Bret *approaches.*)

How is it with our friend?

LE BRET

        Badly.

DE GUICHE

                Indeed?

ROXANE

    (*To* De Guiche)

Oh, he exaggerates!

LE BRET

        Just as I said—
Loneliness, misery—I told him so!—
His satires make a host of enemies—
He attacks the false nobles, the false saints,
The false heroes, the false artists—in short,
Everyone!

ROXANE

        But they fear that sword of his—
No one dare touch him!

DE GUICHE

    (*With a shrug*)

             H'm—that may be so.

LE BRET

It is not violence I fear for him,
But solitude—poverty—old gray December,

Stealing on wolf's feet, with a wolf's green eyes,
Into his darkening room. Those bravoes yet
May strike our Swordsman down! Every day now,
He draws his belt up one hole; his poor nose
Looks like old ivory; he has one coat
Left—his old black serge.

DE GUICHE

That is nothing strange
In this world! No, you need not pity him
Overmuch.

LE BRET

(*With a bitter smile*)
My lord Marshal! . . .

DE GUICHE

I say, do not
Pity him overmuch. He lives his life,
His own life, his own way—thought, word, and deed
Free!

LE BRET

(*As before*)
My lord Duke! . . .

DE GUICHE

(*Haughtily*)
Yes, I know—I have all;
He has nothing. Nevertheless, to-day
I should be proud to shake his hand . . .
(*Saluting* ROXANE)

Adieu.

ROXANE

I will go with you.

(DE GUICHE *salutes* LE BRET, *and turns with* ROX-
ANE *toward the steps.*)

DE GUICHE
(*Pauses on the steps, as she climbs.*)
Yes— I envy him
Now and then . . .

Do you know, when a man wins
Everything in this world, when he succeeds
Too much—he feels, having done nothing wrong
Especially, Heaven knows!—he feels somehow
A thousand small displeasures with himself,
Whose whole sum is not quite Remorse, but rather
A sort of vague disgust . . . The ducal robes
Mounting up, step by step, to pride and power,
Somewhere among their folds draw after them
A rustle of dry illusions, vain regrets
As your veil, up the stairs here, draws along
The whisper of dead leaves.

ROXANE

(*Ironical*)   The sentiment
Does you honor.

DE GUICHE
Oh, yes . . .
(*Pausing suddenly.*)
Monsieur Le Bret!—
(*To* ROXANE)
You pardon us?—

(*He goes to* Le Bret, *and speaks in a low tone.*)
                    One moment— It is true
That no one dares attack your friend. Some people
Dislike him, none the less. The other day
At Court, such a one said to me: "This man
Cyrano may die—accidentally."

LE BRET

(*Coldly*)
Thank you.

DE GUICHE

                    You may thank me. Keep him at home
All you can. Tell him to be careful.

LE BRET

(*Shaking his hands to heaven.*)
                              Careful!—
He is coming here. I'll warn him—yes, but! . . .

ROXANE

(*Still on the steps, to a Nun who approaches her*)
                                        Here
I am—what is it?

THE NUN

Madame, Ragueneau
Wishes to see you.

ROXANE

Bring him here.
        (*To* Le Bret *and* De Guiche)
                              He comes
For sympathy—having been first of all

A Poet, he became since then, in turn,
A Singer—

LE BRET
Bath-house keeper—

ROXANE

                                        Sacristan—

LE BRET
Actor—

ROXANE
            Hairdresser—

LE BRET
                    Music-master—

ROXANE

                                                Now,

To-day—

RAGUENEAU
        (*Enters hurriedly.*)
            Madame!—
        (*He sees* LE BRET.)

                        Monsieur!—

ROXANE
        (*Smiling*)

                            First tell your troubles
To Le Bret for a moment.

RAGUENEAU
                But, Madame—
        (*She goes out, with* DE GUICHE, *not hearing him.*
        RAGUENEAU *comes to* LE BRET.)

After all, I had rather— You are here—
She need not know so soon— I went to see him
Just now— Our friend— As I came near his door,
I saw him coming out. I hurried on
To join him. At the corner of the street,
As he passed— Could it be an accident?—
I wonder!—At the window overhead,
A lackey with a heavy log of wood
Let it fall—

LE BRET

Cyrano!

RAGUENEAU

I ran to him—

LE BRET

God! The cowards!

RAGUENEAU

I found him lying there—

A great hole in his head—

LE BRET

Is he alive?

RAGUENEAU

Alive—yes. But . . . I had to carry him
Up to his room—Dieu! Have you seen his room?—

LE BRET

Is he suffering?

RAGUENEAU

No; unconscious.

LE BRET

Did you

Call a doctor?

RAGUENEAU

One came—for charity.

LE BRET

Poor Cyrano!—We must not tell Roxane
All at once . . . Did the doctor say?—

RAGUENEAU

He said

Fever, and lesions of the— I forget
Those long names— Ah, if you had seen him there,
His head all white bandages!—Let us go
Quickly—there is no one to care for him—
All alone— If he tries to raise his head,
He may die!

LE BRET

(*Draws him away to the Right.*)

This way— It is shorter—through
The Chapel—

ROXANE

(*Appears on the stairway, and calls to* Le Bret *as
he is going out by the colonnade which leads to
the small door of the Chapel.*)

Monsieur Le Bret!—

(Le Bret *and* Ragueneau *rush off without hearing.*)

Running away

When I call to him? Poor dear Ragueneau

Must have been very tragic!

>   (*She comes slowly down the stair, toward the tree.*)
>   What a day! . . .

Something in these bright Autumn afternoons
Happy and yet regretful—an old sorrow
Smiling . . . as though poor little April dried
Her tears long ago—and remembered . . .

>   (*She sits down at her work. Two Nuns come out
>   of the house carrying a great chair and set it
>   under the tree.*)

>   Ah—

The old chair, for my old friend!—

SISTER MARTHE

>   The best one

In our best parlor!—

ROXANE

>   Thank you, Sister—
>   (*The Nuns withdraw.*)

>   There—

>   (*She begins embroidering. The clock strikes.*)

The hour!—He will be coming now—my silks—
All done striking? He never was so late
Before! The sister at the door—my thimble . . .
Here it is—she must be exhorting him
To repent all his sins . . .

>   (*A pause*)

>   He ought to be

Converted, by this time— Another leaf—

>   (*A dead leaf falls on her work; she brushes it
>   away.*)

Certainly nothing could—my scissors—ever
Keep him away—

A NUN

(*Appears on the steps.*)
                Monsieur de Bergerac.

ROXANE

(*Without turning*)
What was I saying? . . . Hard, sometimes, to match
These faded colors! . . .

(*While she goes on working,* CYRANO *appears at
the top of the steps, very pale, his hat drawn over
his eyes. The Nun who has brought him in goes
away. He begins to descend the steps leaning on
his cane, and holding himself on his feet only by
an evident effort.* ROXANE *turns to him, with a
tone of friendly banter.*)
                        After fourteen years,
Late—for the first time!

CYRANO

(*Reaches the chair, and sinks into it; his gay tone
contrasting with his tortured face.*)
                    Yes, yes—maddening!
I was detained by—

ROXANE
    Well?

CYRANO
            A visitor,
Most unexpected.

ROXANE

(*Carelessly, still sewing*)
                    Was your visitor
Tiresome?

CYRANO

              Why, hardly that—inopportune,
Let us say—an old friend of mine—at least
A very old acquaintance.

ROXANE

                          Did you tell him
To go away?

CYRANO

              For the time being, yes.
I said: "Excuse me—this is Saturday—
I have a previous engagement, one
I cannot miss, even for you— Come back
An hour from now."

ROXANE

                    Your friend will have to wait;
I shall not let you go till dark.

CYRANO

(*Very gently*)
                          Perhaps
A little before dark, I must go . . .
        (*He leans back in the chair, and closes his eyes.
        SISTER MARTHE crosses above the stairway. ROX-
        ANE sees her, motions her to wait, then turns to
        CYRANO.*)

ROXANE

Look—

Somebody waiting to be teased.

CYRANO
                    (*Quickly, opens his eyes.*)
                                        Of course!
        (*In a big, comic voice*)
Sister, approach!
            (SISTER MARTHE *glides toward him.*)
                    Beautiful downcast eyes!—
So shy—

SISTER MARTHE
            (*Looks up, smiling.*)
        You—
            (*She sees his face.*)
                    Oh!—

CYRANO
        (*Indicates* ROXANE.)
                            Sh!—Careful!
        (*Resumes his burlesque tone.*)
                                        Yesterday,
I ate meat again!

SISTER MARTHE
            Yes, I know.
    (*Aside*)
                            That is why
He looks so pale . . .
        (*To him: low and quickly*)
                    In the refectory,

Before you go—come to me there—

                            I'll make you

A great bowl of hot soup—will you come?

CYRANO

    (*Boisterously*)

                                  Ah—

Will I come!

SISTER MARTHE

          You are quite reasonable

To-day!

ROXANE

         Has she converted you?

SISTER MARTHE

                      Oh, no—

Not for the world!—

CYRANO

               Why, now I think of it,

That is so— You, bursting with holiness,

And yet you never preach! Astonishing

I call it . . .

    (*With burlesque ferocity*)

             Ah—now I'll astonish you—

I am going to—

      (*With the air of seeking for a good joke and find-*
        ing it)

               —let you pray for me

To-night, at vespers!

ROXANE

      Aha!

CYRANO

Look at her—

Absolutely struck dumb!

SISTER MARTHE

(*Gently*)

I did not wait

For you to say I might.
(*She goes out.*)

CYRANO

(*Returns to* ROXANE, *who is bending over her work.*)

Now, may the devil

Admire me, if I ever hope to see
The end of that embroidery!

ROXANE

(*Smiling*)

I thought

It was time you said that.
(*A breath of wind causes a few leaves to fall.*)

CYRANO

The leaves—

ROXANE

(*Raises her head and looks away through the trees.*)

What color—

Perfect Venetian red! Look at them fall.

CYRANO

Yes—they know how to die. A little way
From the branch to the earth, a little fear

Of mingling with the common dust—and yet
They go down gracefully—a fall that seems
Like flying!

ROXANE

Melancholy—you?

CYRANO

Why, no,
Roxane!

ROXANE

Then let the leaves fall. Tell me now
The Court news—my Gazette!

CYRANO

Let me see—

ROXANE

Ah!

CYRANO

(More and more pale, struggling against pain)
Saturday, the nineteenth: The King fell ill,
After eight helpings of grape marmalade.
His malady was brought before the court,
Found guilty of high treason; whereupon
His Majesty revived. The royal pulse
Is now normal. Sunday, the twentieth:
The Queen gave a grand ball, at which they burned
Seven hundred and sixty-three wax candles. Note:
They say our troops have been victorious
In Austria. Later: Three sorcerers
Have been hung. Special post: The little dog

Of Madame d'Athis was obliged to take
Four pills before—

ROXANE

Monsieur de Bergerac,
Will you kindly be quiet!

CYRANO

Monday . . . nothing.
Lygdamire has a new lover.

ROXANE

Oh,

CYRANO

(*His face more and more altered*)

Tuesday,
The Twenty-second: All the court has gone
To Fontainebleau. *Wednesday:* The Comte de Fiesque
Spoke to Madame de Montglat; she said No.
Thursday: Mancini was the Queen of France
Or—very nearly! *Friday:* La Montglat
Said Yes. *Saturday twenty-sixth.* . . .

(*His eyes close; his head sinks back; silence.*)

ROXANE

(*Surprised at not hearing any more, turns, looks at
him, and rises, frightened.*)

He has fainted—

(*She runs to him, crying out.*)

Cyrano!

CYRANO

(*Opens his eyes.*)

What . . . What is it? . . .

(He sees ROXANE *leaning over him, and quickly pulls his hat down over his head and leans back away from her in the chair.)*

No—oh no—

It is nothing—truly!

ROXANE

But—

CYRANO

My old wound—

At Arras—sometimes—you know. . . .

ROXANE

My poor friend!

CYRANO

Oh it is nothing; it will soon be gone. . . .
(Forcing a smile)
There! It is gone!

ROXANE

(Standing close to him)
We all have our old wounds—

I have mine—here . . .
(Her hand at her breast)
under this faded scrap

Of writing. . . . It is hard to read now—all
But the blood—and the tears. . . .
(Twilight begins to fall.)

CYRANO

His letter! . . . Did you

Not promise me that some day . . . that some day
You would let me read it?

ROXANE

His letter?—You . . .
You wish—

CYRANO

I do wish it—to-day.

ROXANE

(*Gives him the little silken bag from around her neck.*)

Here. . . .

CYRANO

May I . . . open it?

ROXANE

Open it, and read.
(*She goes back to her work, folds it again, rearranges her silks.*)

CYRANO

(*Unfolds the letter; reads.*)
'Farewell Roxane, because to-day I die—"

ROXANE

(*Looks up, surprised.*)
Aloud?

CYRANO

(*Reads*)
    "I know that it will be to-day,
My own dearly beloved—and my heart
Still so heavy with love I have not told,
And I die without telling you! No more
Shall my eyes drink the sight of you like wine,

Never more, with a look that is a kiss,
Follow the sweet grace of you—"

ROXANE

How you read it—
His letter!

CYRANO

(*Continues*)
"I remember now the way
You have, of pushing back a lock of hair
With one hand, from your forehead—and my heart
Cries out—"

ROXANE

His letter . . . and you read it so . . .
(*The darkness increases imperceptibly.*)

CYRANO

"Cries out and keeps crying: 'Farewell, my dear,
My dearest—' "

ROXANE

In a voice. . . .

CYRANO

"—My own heart's own,
My own treasure—"

ROXANE

(*Dreamily*)

In such a voice. . . .

CYRANO

—"My love—"

ROXANE

—As I remember hearing . . .
　　　(*She trembles.*)

　　　　　　　　　　　　　—long ago. . . .
　　　(*She comes near him, softly, without his seeing her;
　　　passes the chair, leans over silently, looking at the
　　　letter. The darkness increases.*)

CYRANO

"—I am never away from you. Even now,
I shall not leave you. In another world,
I shall be still that one who loves you, loves **you**
Beyond measure, beyond—"

ROXANE

　　　(*Lays her hand on his shoulder.*)
　　　　　　　　　　　　How can you read
Now? It is dark. . . .
　　　(*He starts, turns, and sees her there close to him.
　　　A little movement of surprise, almost of fear;
　　　then he bows his head.
　　　A long pause; then in the twilight now completely
　　　fallen, she says very softly, clasping her hands*)
　　　　　　　　　　　　And all these fourteen years,
He has been the old friend, who came to me
To be amusing.

CYRANO

Roxane!—

ROXANE

It was you.

CYRANO

No, no, Roxane, no!

ROXANE

And I might have known,
Every time that I heard you speak my name! . . .

CYRANO

No— It was not I—

ROXANE

It was . . . you!

CYRANO

I swear—

ROXANE

I understand everything now: The letters—
That was you . . .

CYRANO

No!

ROXANE

And the dear, foolish words—
That was you. . . .

CYRANO

No!

ROXANE

And the voice . . . in the dark. . . .
That was . . . you!

CYRANO

On my honor—

ROXANE

And . . . the Soul!—
That was all you.

CYRANO

I never loved you—

ROXANE

Yes,

You loved me.

CYRANO

(*Desperately*)
No— He loved you—

ROXANE

Even now,

You love me!

CYRANO

(*His voice weakens.*)
No!

ROXANE

(*Smiling*)
And why . . . so great a *No?*

CYRANO

No, no, my own dear love, I love you not! . . .
(*Pause*)

ROXANE

How many things have died . . . and are new-born! . . .
Why were you silent for so many years,
All the while, every night and every day,
He gave me nothing—you knew that— You knew
Here, in this letter lying on my breast,
Your tears— You knew they were your tears—

CYRANO

(*Holds the letter out to her.*)

The blood
Was his.

ROXANE

Why do you break that silence now,
To-day?

CYRANO

Why? Oh, because—
(LE BRET *and* RAGUENEAU *enter, running.*)

LE BRET

What recklessness—
I knew it! He is here!

CYRANO

(*Smiling, and trying to rise*)
Well? Here I am!

RAGUENEAU

He has killed himself, Madame, coming here!

ROXANE

He— Oh, God. . . . And that faintness . . . was that?—

CYRANO

No,
Nothing! I did not finish my Gazette—
Saturday, twenty-sixth: An hour or so
Before dinner, Monsieur de Bergerac
Died, foully murdered.

(*He uncovers his head, and shows it swathed in
bandages.*)

ROXANE

                Oh, what does he mean?—
Cyrano!—What have they done to you?—

CYRANO

                          "Struck down

By the sword of a hero, let me fall—
Steel in my heart, and laughter on my lips!"
Yes, I said that once. How Fate loves a jest!—
Behold me ambushed—taken in the rear—
My battlefield a gutter—my noble foe
A lackey, with a log of wood! . . .

                          It seems
Too logical— I have missed everything,
Even my death!

RAGUENEAU

        (*Breaks down.*)
                Ah, Monsieur!—

CYRANO

                        Ragueneau,
Stop blubbering!
        (*Takes his hand.*)
                What are you writing nowadays,
Old poet?

RAGUENEAU

        (*Through his tears*)
                I am not a poet now;
I snuff the—light the candles—for Molière!

CYRANO

Oh—Molière!

RAGUENEAU

Yes, but I am leaving him
To-morrow. Yesterday they played *Scapin*—
He has stolen your scene—

LE BRET

The whole scene—word for word!

RAGUENEAU

Yes: "What the devil was he doing there"—
That one!

LE BRET

(*Furious*)

And Molière stole it all from you—
Bodily!—

CYRANO

Bah— He showed good taste. . . .
(*To* RAGUENEAU)

The Scene

Went well? . . .

RAGUENEAU

Ah, Monsieur, they laughed—and laughed—
How they did laugh!

CYRANO

Yes—that has been my life
Do you remember that night Christian spoke
Under your window? It was always so!
While I stood in the darkness underneath,
Others climbed up to win the applause—the kiss!—
Well—that seems only justice— I still say,
Even now, on the threshold of my tomb—

"Molière has genius—Christian had good looks—"

> (*The chapel bell is ringing. Along the avenue of trees above the stairway, the Nuns pass in procession to their prayers.*)

They are going to pray now; there is the bell.

ROXANE

> (*Raises herself and calls to them.*)

Sister!—Sister!—

CYRANO

> (*Holding on to her hand*)
>
> No,—do not go away—

I may not still be here when you return. . . .

> (*The Nuns have gone into the chapel. The organ begins to play.*)

A little harmony is all I need—

Listen. . . .

ROXANE

You shall not die! I love you!—

CYRANO

No—

That is not in the story! You remember
When Beauty said "I love you" to the Beast
That was a fairy prince, his ugliness
Changed and dissolved, like magic. . . . But you see
I am still the same.

ROXANE

And I—I have done

This to you! All my fault—mine!

CYRANO

You? Why, no,
On the contrary! I had never known
Womanhood and its sweetness but for you.
My mother did not love to look at me—
I never had a sister— Later on,
I feared the mistress with a mockery
Behind her smile. But you—because of you
I have had one friend not quite all a friend—
Across my life, one whispering silken gown! . . .

LE BRET

(*Points to the rising moon which begins to shine
down between the trees.*)
Your other friend is looking at you.

CYRANO

(*Smiling at the moon*)

I see. . . .

ROXANE

I never loved but one man in my life,
And I have lost him—twice. . . .

CYRANO

Le Bret—I shall be up there presently
In the moon—without having to invent
Any flying-machines!

ROXANE

What are you saying? . . .

CYRANO

The moon—yes, that would be the place for me—
My kind of paradise! I shall find there

Those other souls who should be friends of mine—
Socrates—Galileo—

LE BRET

(*Revolting*)

No! No! No!

It is too idiotic—too unfair—
Such a friend—such a poet—such a man
To die so—to die so!—

CYRANO

(*Affectionately*)

There goes Le Bret,

Growling!

LE BRET

(*Breaks down.*)

My friend!—

CYRANO

(*Half raises himself, his eye wanders.*)

The Cadets of Gascoyne,

The Defenders. . . . The elementary mass—
Ah—there's the point! Now, then . . .

LE BRET

Delirious—

And all that learning—

CYRANO

On the other hand,

We have Copernicus—

ROXANE

Oh!

CYRANO

(*More and more delirious*)

"Very well,
But what the devil was he doing there?—
What the devil was he doing there, up there?" . . .

(*He declaims.*)

Philosopher and scientist,
Poet, musician, duellist—
  He flew high, and fell back again!
A pretty wit—whose like we lack—
A lover . . . not like other men. . . .
  Here lies Hercule-Savinien
De Cyrano de Bergerac—
  Who was all things—and all in vain!

Well, I must go—pardon— I cannot stay!
My moonbeam comes to carry me away. . . .

(*He falls back into the chair, half fainting. The
sobbing of* ROXANE *recalls him to reality. Grad-
ually his mind comes back to him. He looks at
her, stroking the veil that hides her hair.*)

I would not have you mourn any the less
That good, brave, noble Christian; but perhaps—
I ask you only this—when the great cold
Gathers around my bones, that you may give
A double meaning to your widow's weeds
And the tears you let fall for him may be
For a little—my tears. . . .

ROXANE

(*Sobbing*)

Oh, my love! . . .

CYRANO

(*Suddenly shaken as with a fever fit, he raises himself erect and pushes her away.*)

—Not here!—

Not lying down! . . .

(*They spring forward to help him; he motions
them back.*)

Let no one help me—no one!—

Only the tree. . . .

(*He sets his back against the trunk. Pause.*)

It is coming . . . I feel
Already shod with marble . . . gloved with lead . . .

(*Joyously*)

Let the old fellow come now! He shall find me
On my feet—sword in hand—

(*Draws his sword.*)

LE BRET

Cyrano!—

ROXANE

(*Half fainting*)

Oh,

Cyrano!

CYRANO

I can see him there—he grins—
He is looking at my nose—that skeleton
—What's that you say? Hopeless?—Why, very well!—
But a man does not fight merely to win!
No—no—better to know one fights in vain! . . .
You there— Who are you? A hundred against one—

I know them now, my ancient enemies—
    (*He lunges at the empty air.*)
Falsehood! . . . There! There! Prejudice— Compro-
    mise—
Cowardice—
    (*Thrusting*)
              What's that? No! Surrender? No!
Never—never! . . .
                Ah, you too, Vanity!
I knew you would overthrow me in the end—
No! I fight on! I fight on! I fight on!
    (*He swings the blade in great circles, then pauses,
        gasping. When he speaks again, it is another
        tone.*)
Yes, all my laurels you have riven away
And all my roses; yet in spite of you,
There is one crown I bear away with me,
And to-night, when I enter before God,
My salute shall sweep all the stars away
From the blue threshold! One thing without stain,
Unspotted from the world, in spite of doom
Mine own!—
    (*He springs forward, his sword aloft.*)
         And that is . . .
    (*The sword escapes from his hand; he totters, and
        falls into the arms of* LE BRET *and* RAGUENEAU.)

ROXANE
(*Bends over him and kisses him on the forehead.*)
        —That is . . .

CYRANO

(Opens his eyes and smiles up at her.)

My white plume. . . .

(Curtain)

Modern Library of the World's Best Books

COMPLETE LIST OF TITLES IN

THE MODERN LIBRARY

For convenience in ordering use number at right of title